BROOKINGS INSTITUTION, WASHINGTON, D.C.
INSTITUTE FOR GOVERNMENT RESEARCH

SERVICE MONOGRAPHS
OF THE
UNITED STATES GOVERNMENT
No. 3

THE BUREAU OF MINES
ITS HISTORY, ACTIVITIES AND ORGANIZATION

AMS PRESS
NEW YORK

THE INSTITUTE FOR GOVERNMENT RESEARCH
Washington, D. C.

The Institute for Government Research is an association of citizens for coöperating with public officials in the scientific study of government with a view to promoting efficiency and economy in its operations and advancing the science of administration. It aims to bring into existence such information and materials as will aid in the formation of public opinion and will assist officials, particularly those of the national government, in their efforts to put the public administration upon a more efficient basis.

To this end, it seeks by the thoroughgoing study and examination of the best administrative practice, public and private, American and foreign, to formulate those principles which lie at the basis of all sound administration, and to determine their proper adaptation to the specific needs of our public administration.

The accomplishment of specific reforms the Institute recognizes to be the task of those who are charged with the responsibility of legislation and administration; but it seeks to assist, by scientific study and research, in laying a solid foundation of information and experience upon which such reforms may be successfully built.

While some of the Institute's studies find application only in the form of practical coöperation with the administrative officers directly concerned, many are of interest to other administrators and of general educational value. The results of such studies the Institute purposes to publish in such form as will insure for them the widest possible utilization.

Officers

Robert S. Brookings, *Chairman*
James F. Curtis, *Secretary*
Frank J. Goodnow, *Vice-Chairman*
Frederick Strauss, *Treasurer*

Trustees

Edwin A. Alderman
Robert S. Brookings
James F. Curtis
R. Fulton Cutting
Frederic A. Delano
George Eastman
Raymond B. Fosdick
Felix Frankfurter
Edwin F. Gay
Frank J. Goodnow
Jerome D. Greene
Arthur T. Hadley
Herbert C. Hoover
A. Lawrence Lowell
Samuel Mather
Richard B. Mellon
Charles D. Norton
Martin A. Ryerson
Frederick Strauss
Silas H. Strawn
William H. Taft
Ray Lyman Wilbur
Robert S. Woodward

Director
W. F. Willoughby

Editor
F. W. Powell

INSTITUTE FOR GOVERNMENT RESEARCH

SERVICE MONOGRAPHS
OF THE
UNITED STATES GOVERNMENT
No. 3

THE BUREAU OF MINES

ITS HISTORY, ACTIVITIES AND ORGANIZATION

BY
FRED WILBUR POWELL

D. APPLETON AND COMPANY
NEW YORK   LONDON
1922

Library of Congress Cataloging in Publication Data

Powell, Fred Wilbur, 1881-1943.
  The Bureau of Mines.

  Original ed. issued as no. 3 of Service monographs of the United States Government.
  Bibliography: p.
  1. United States. Bureau of Mines. I. Series: Brookings Institution, Washington, D.C. Institute for Government Research. Service monographs of the United States Government, no. 3.
  TN23.P6   1974   353.008'238   72-3016
  ISBN 0-404-57103-4

Reprinted, with permission, from a volume in the collections of the Newark Public Library

Reprinted from the edition of 1922, New York and London
First AMS edition published, 1974
Manufactured in the United States of America

International Standard Book Number:
Complete Set: 0-404-57100-X
Volume 3: 0-404-57103-4

AMS Press, Inc.
New York, N.Y. 10003

PUBLICATIONS OF THE
INSTITUTE FOR GOVERNMENT RESEARCH

STUDIES IN ADMINISTRATION
The System of Financial Administration of Great Britain
By W. F. Willoughby, W. W. Willoughby, and S. M. Lindsay
The Budget
By René Stourm
T. Plazinski, Translator; W. F. McCaleb, Editor
The Canadian Budgetary System
By H. G. Villard and W. W. Willoughby
The Problem of a National Budget
By W. F. Willoughby
The Movement for Budgetary Reform in the States
By W. F. Willoughby
Teacher's Pension Systems in the United States
By Paul Studensky
Organized Efforts for the Improvement of Methods of Administration in the United States
By Gustavus A. Weber
The Federal Service: A Study of the System of Personal Administration of the United States Government
By Lewis Mayers
The System of Financial Administration of the United States

PRINCIPLES OF ADMINISTRATION
Principles Governing the Retirement of Public Employees
By Lewis Meriam
Principles of Government Purchasing
By Arthur G. Thomas
Principles of Government Accounting and Reporting
By Francis Oakey, C. P. A.
Principles of Personnel Administration
By Arthur W. Procter

SERVICE MONOGRAPHS OF THE UNITED STATES GOVERNMENT
The Geological Survey
The Reclamation Service
The Bureau of Mines
The Alaskan Engineering Commission
The Tariff Commission
The Federal Board for Vocational Education
The Federal Trade Commission
The Steamboat-Inspection Service
The National Parks Service
The Public Health Service
The Weather Bureau
The Employee's Compensation Commission

352961

FOREWORD

The first essential to efficient administration of any enterprise is full knowledge of its present make-up and operation. Without full and complete information before them, as to existing organization, personnel, plant, and methods of operation and control, neither legislators nor administrators can properly perform their functions.

The greater the work, the more varied the activities engaged in, and the more complex the organization employed, and more imperative becomes the necessity that this information shall be available—and available in such a form that it can readily be utilized.

Of all undertakings, none in the United States, and few, if any, in the world, approach in magnitude, complexity, and importance that of the national government of the United States. As President Taft expressed it in his message to Congress of January 17, 1912, in referring to the inquiry being made under his direction into the efficiency and economy of the methods of prosecuting public business, the activities of the national government "are almost as varied as those of the entire business world. The operations of the government affect the interest of every person living within the jurisdiction of the United States. Its organization embraces stations and centers of work located in every city and in many local subdivisions of the country. Its gross expenditures amount to billions annually. Including the personnel of the military and naval establishments, more than half a million persons are required to do the work imposed by law upon the executive branch of the government.

"This vast organization has never been studied in detail as one piece of administrative mechanism. Never have the foundations been laid for a thorough consideration of the relations of all its parts. No comprehensive effort has been made to list its multifarious activities or to group them in such a way as to present a clear picture of what the government is doing. Never has a complete description been given of the agencies through which these activities are performed. At no time has the attempt been made to study all of these activities and agencies with a view to the assignment of each activity to the agency best fitted for its performance, to the avoidance of duplication of plant and work, to the integration of all administrative agencies of the government, so far as may be practicable, into a unified organization for the most effective and economical dispatch of public business."

To lay the basis for such a comprehensive study of the organization and operations of the national government as President Taft outlined, the Institute for Government Research has undertaken the preparation of a series of monographs, of which the present study is one, giving a detailed description of each of the fifty or more distinct services of the government. These studies are being vigorously prosecuted, and it is hoped that all services of the government will be covered in a comparatively brief space of time. Thereafter, revisions of the monographs will be made from time to time as need arises, to the end that they may, as far as practicable, represent current conditions.

These monographs are all prepared according to a uniform plan. They give: first, the history of the establishment and development of the service; second, its functions, described not in general terms, but by detailing its specific activities; third, its organization for the handling of these activities; fourth, the character of its plant; fifth, a compilation of, or reference to, the laws and regulations governing its operations; sixth, financial statements showing its appropriations, expenditures and other data for a period of years; and finally, a full bibliography of the sources of information, official and private, bearing on the service and its operations.

In the preparation of these monographs the Institute has kept steadily in mind the aim to produce documents that will be of direct value and assistance in the administration of public affairs. To executive officials they offer valuable tools of administration. Through them, such officers can, with a minimum of effort, inform themselves regarding the details, not only of their own services, but of others with whose facilities, activities, and methods it is desirable that they should be familiar. Under present conditions services frequently engage in activities in ignorance of the fact that the work projected has already been done, or is in process of execution by other services. Many cases exist where one service could make effective use of the organization, plant or results of other services had they knowledge that such facilities were in existence. With the constant shifting of directing personnel that takes place in the administrative branch of the national government, the existence of means by which incoming officials may thus readily secure information regarding their own and other services is a matter of great importance.

To members of Congress the monographs should prove of no less value. At present these officials are called upon to legislate and appropriate money for services concerning whose needs and real problems they can secure but imperfect information. That the possession by each member of a set of monographs, such as is here projected, prepared according to a uniform plan, will be a great aid to intelligent legislation and appropriation of funds can hardly be questioned.

To the public, finally, these monographs will give that knowledge of the organization and operations of their government which must be had if an enlightened public opinion is to be brought to bear upon the conduct of governmental affairs.

These studies are wholly descriptive in character. No attempt is made in them to subject the conditions described to criticism, nor to indicate features in respect to which changes might with advantage be made. Upon administrators themselves falls responsibility for making or proposing changes which will result in the improvement of methods of administration. The primary aim of outside agencies should be to emphasize this responsibility and facilitate its fulfillment.

While the monographs thus make no direct recommendations for improvement, they cannot fail greatly to stimulate efforts in that direction. Prepared as they are according to a uniform plan, and setting forth as they do the activities, plant, organization, personnel and laws governing the several services of the government, they will automatically, as it were, reveal, for example, the extent to which work in the same field is being performed by different services, and thus furnish the information that is essential to a consideration of the great question of the better distribution and coördination of activities among the several departments, establishments, and bureaus, and the elimination of duplications of plant, organization and work. Through them it will also be possible to subject any particular feature of the administrative work of the government to exhaustive study, to determine, for example, what facilities, in the way of laboratories and other plant and equipment, exist for the prosecution of any line of work and where those facilities are located; or what work is being done in any field of administration or research, such as the promotion, protection and regulation of the maritime interests of the country, the planning and execution of works of an engineering character, or the collection, compilation and publication of statistical data, or what differences of practice prevail in respect to organization, classification, appointment, and promotion of personnel.

To recapitulate, the monographs will serve the double purpose of furnishing an essential tool for efficient legislation, administration and popular control, and of laying the basis for critical and constructive work on the part of those upon whom responsibility for such work primarily rests.

Whenever possible the language of official statements or reports has been employed, and it has not been practicable in all cases to make specific indication of the language so quoted.

CONTENTS

CHAPTER		PAGE
	FOREWORD	
I.	HISTORY	1
	Mining Technological Work of Geological Survey	1
	Creation and Development of the Bureau of Mines	3
II.	ACTIVITIES	7
	Promotion of Safety and Health	8
	Investigation of accidents	8
	Research in accident prevention	8
	Investigation of mine hazards	11
	Investigation of hygienic conditions	11
	Operation of mine-rescue stations and cars	13
	Publicity	15
	Technological Researches and Investigations	16
	Mining	16
	Mineral technology	20
	Metallurgy	21
	Solid mineral fuels	22
	Petroleum and natural gas	25
	Coöperation	29
	Administration	31
	Inspection of mines and mine leases	31
	Mineral land leases	32
	Explosives regulation	33
	Utilization of surplus War Department explosives	33
	War minerals relief	34
	Operation of the Government Fuel Yard	34
	Compilation of Mining Laws and Regulations	35
	War Activities	35
III.	ORGANIZATION	37
	General Administration	39
	Office proper of the director	39
	Office of the assistant director	39
	Office of the assistant to the director	39
	Operations Branch	39
	Division of office administration	39
	Personnel	40
	Accounts	40
	Legal	40
	Mails and files	40
	Property and shipments	41
	Mimeograph	41
	Division of education and information	41
	Editorial	42

CONTENTS

CHAPTER	PAGE
Publications	42
Motion pictures and exhibits	43
Statistics	43
Codification of mining laws	43
Library	43
Reference files	43
Division of mine-rescue cars and stations	43
Safety districts	44
Rescue stations	44
Rescue cars	44
Government fuel yard	45
Investigations Branch	45
Chief surgeon	46
Mining division	46
Division of mineral technology	47
Metallurgical division	48
Fuels division	48
Division of petroleum and natural gas	49
Division of mining experiment stations	49
Experiment stations	50

APPENDIX

1. Outline of Organization 51
2. Classification of Activities 70
3. **Publications** 72
4. Plant and Equipment 76
5. Laws 82
   Index to laws 82
   Compilation of laws 85
6. Financial Statements 136
   Appropriations 136
   Expenditures 137
   Repayments 137
   Miscellaneous receipts 137
7. Bibliography 146

Index 161

THE BUREAU OF MINES: ITS HISTORY, ACTIVITIES AND ORGANIZATION

CHAPTER I

HISTORY

The Bureau of Mines was created in 1910 as a part of the Department of the Interior to conduct inquiries and investigations calculated to increase health, safety, economy, and efficiency in the mining, quarrying, metallurgical, and miscellaneous mineral industries of the country.

While some of the interests of these industries had been served by the United States Geological Survey from its inception in 1879, there was a growing demand for special recognition and aid from the national government, particularly among the metal-mining interests in the western states and the eastern bituminous coal mining industry. This movement first became articulate in 1896 when, at its first annual convention at Denver, the American Mining Congress proposed the creation of a national department of mines with representation in the President's cabinet. From time to time thereafter bills for the establishment of a separate organization were introduced into Congress with the ultimate result set forth in the foregoing paragraph.

Mining Technological Work of Geological Survey. From the first the Geological Survey had established a close relation to the mining and mineral industries through the preparation of its annual report on "Mineral Resources of the United States." This relation was steadily strengthened by investigations made by the Survey in important mining areas, by investigations and publications relative to technologic processes, beginning in 1894, and by the publication of parts of a geologic map of the country, most of the early issues of which covered areas of interest to the mining industry. In 1899 a systematic inquiry into the value of the several deposits of economic minerals was proposed by the Director of the Geological Survey as a task which might well be undertaken by a division of mines and mining, the establishment of which he recommended.

The first effective response to this suggestion came in 1904 (Act of February 18, 1904; 33 Stat. L., 15, 33) when Congress appropriated $30,000 for analyzing and testing the coals of the United States. In 1905 this appropriation was enlarged to $227,000 and its provisions were extended to cover all fuels (Act of January 5, 1905; 33 Stat. L., 602,603, and act of March 3, 1905; 33 Stat. L., 1156, 1187). Another appropriation provided for an investigation of structural materials.

In connection with both investigations the Geological Survey was called upon to give expert advice as to fuels and structural materials to other branches of the national government; and the preparation of specifications and the testing of fuels and materials came to be a standing feature of its work.

Under the act of 1904 the work of fuel-testing was begun at the Louisiana Purchase Exposition at St. Louis under the direction of Dr. Joseph A. Holmes. It was continued at St. Louis until 1907 when the equipment was removed; part of it going to the Jamestown Exposition at Norfolk and part to Denver. Other fuel-testing laboratories were established at Columbus, Pittsburgh, and Washington (Act of June 30, 1906, 34 Stat. L., 697, 728; act of March 4, 1907, 34 Stat. L., 1275, 1335; act of May 27, 1908, 35 Stat. L., 317, 349; and act of March 4, 1909, 35 Stat. L., 945, 989).

By an order dated April 2, 1907 the Secretary of the Interior established a Technologic Branch in the Geological Sur-

HISTORY

vey to conduct the work of testing fuels and structural materials, and appointed Dr. Holmes Chief Technologist. The duties of the new branch were extended by an act passed in 1908 (Act of May 22, 1908; 35 Stat. L., 184, 226. See also act of March 4, 1909; 35 Stat. L., 945, 989), which appropriated $150,000 "for the protection of lives of miners in the territories and in the District of Alaska, and for conducting investigations as to the causes of mine explosions with a view to increasing safety in mining." This was in part the result of the representations of the American Mining Congress, but the immediate cause was the awakened interest of Congress following a series of disastrous coal mine explosions in December, 1907.

Under this appropriation the Technologic Branch made examinations of explosives used in coal mines and of safety lamps and mine-rescue apparatus. It also conducted inquiries into the occurrence of explosive gases and inflammable or explosive dusts and into the use of electricity in mines. This work was done chiefly at Pittsburgh, (Pa.). Stations equipped with mine-rescue apparatus were established at Pittsburgh, (Pa.) and Urbana, (Ill.) in 1908, and additional stations were established in 1909 at Knoxville and at Seattle. These stations were equipped with mine-rescue apparatus, and manned with a personnel trained in first-aid and rescue methods. By this means it was possible to afford immediate aid after mine explosions and to train miners in first-aid methods and for rescue work following mine disasters.

Creation and Development of Bureau of Mines. For the fiscal year 1908-09 the appropriations for the three classes of technologic investigations—testing of fuels, testing of structural materials, and investigation of mine explosives—had reached a total of over $500,000; and although the appropriation for fuel-testing was reduced the next year, it became apparent that the investigation of mining accidents would increase both in cost and in importance. The lack of close connection between this engineering type of investigation and the regular geologic work of the Geological Survey, the growing realization of the waste of both life and resources in the mining and metallurgical industries, and the insistence of the organized mining interests of the country that they be given definite representation in the national government, led to the proposal that a Bureau of Mines be created as a coördinate branch of the Department of the Interior and charged with the conduct and development of the mining technologic work begun by the Geological Survey. The result was an act passed in 1910 (Act of May 6, 1910; 36 Stat. L., 369) establishing the Bureau of Mines.

This act authorized the Secretary of the Interior to transfer to the new bureau the three types of investigations hitherto conducted by the Technologic Branch of the Geological Survey, together with the property, equipment, and personnel connected therewith. It became effective July 1, 1910, and Dr. Holmes was appointed Director after a short interval. Dr. Holmes continued to direct the work of the bureau until his death in July, 1913. He was succeeded by Van H. Manning, who resigned in June, 1920. Dr. F. G. Cottrell was then appointed to the directorship. He resigned on December 31, 1920 and was succeeded by H. Foster Bain, the present Director.

As defined by the organic act the scope of the Bureau of Mines was extended into the technical processes of production and of utilization, including mineral technology and metallurgy,—fields of investigation which had not been mentioned in any of the appropriation acts for the Geological Survey. Besides the testing of fuels and investigation of mine explosions, taken over from the Geological Survey, it included investigation of the methods of mining, especially in relation to:

    The safety of miners, and the appliances best adapted to prevent accidents;
    The possible improvement of the conditions under which mining operations are carried on;

The treatment of ores and other mineral substances;
The use of explosives and electricity; and
The prevention of accidents.

It also included "other inquiries and technologic investigations pertinent to said industries."

Before it went into effect this act was modified in two particulars (Act of June 25, 1910; 36 Stat. L., 703, 742, 743, 765): the appointment was authorized of two inspectors of coal and other mines in the District of Alaska, pursuant to the act for the protection of the lives of miners in the territories (Act of March 3, 1891: 26 Stat L., 1104), and the supervision of the inspection of structural materials was transferred to the Bureau of Standards of the Department of Commerce and Labor.

In 1911 provision was made (Act of March 4, 1911; 36 Stat. L., 1363, 1419) for tests or investigations, other than those performed for the national government or a state government, on a fee basis, subject to authorization by the Secretary of the Interior.

The bureau's scope was extended in 1913 by an amendment (Act of February 25, 1913; 37 Stat. 681) which wholly supplanted the original organic act. Here it was described as "a bureau of mining, metallurgy, and mineral technology." One section describes the functions of the bureau as follows:

> To conduct inquiries and scientific and technologic investigations concerning mining, and the preparation, treatment, and utilization of mineral substances, with a view to improving health conditions, and increasing safety, efficiency, economic development, and conserving resources through the prevention of waste in the mining, quarrying, metallurgical, and other mineral industries;
> To inquire into the economic conditions affecting those industries;
> To investigate explosives and peat; and
> On behalf of the government to investigate the mineral fuels and unfinished mineral products belonging to, or for the use of, the United States, with a view to their most efficient mining, preparation, treatment and use.

Another section further elaborates them in the following terms:

> Inquiries and investigations . . . concerning the nature, causes, and prevention of accidents, and the improvement of conditions, methods, and equipment, with special reference to health, safety, and prevention of waste in the mining, quarrying, metallurgical, and other mineral industries; the use of explosives and electricity, safety methods and appliances, and rescue and first-aid work in said industries; the causes and prevention of mine fires. . . .

In 1915 Congress passed an act (Act of March 3, 1915; 38 Stat. L., 959) authorizing the establishment of seven mine safety stations and ten mining experiment stations. By 1921 the number of experiment stations had increased to thirteen, and there were in addition twelve field offices.

From time to time additional duties have been imposed upon the bureau by statute or by orders of the Secretary of the Interior, but except in connection with matters relating to the World War the principal activities have remained as fixed by the act of 1913. In the succeeding chapter those activities are considered in some detail.

CHAPTER II

ACTIVITIES [1]

As has been indicated in the foregoing chapter the Bureau of Mines concerns itself with mining industries of all kinds, that is, with the extraction of mineral substances, whether from mines or quarries or from oil wells. Its interest is not confined merely to extraction from the ground but includes also preparation, treatment, and utilization,—the field of metallurgy. Since the scope of the field is large, it is necessary to have relations with other agencies, and these relations have been established on the following terms:

The bureau conducts the necessary general inquiries and investigations in regard to the mining and metallurgical industries and makes the results available.

Individual states are looked to for enacting legislation and setting up the necessary organization for inspection of mining operations.

Mine, mill, and smelter operators are expected to introduce facilities, methods, and processes demonstrated by the bureau's efforts as efficacious in the elimination of hazardous conditions and waste of valuable materials.

Mine managers and miners are to coöperate in making and enforcing rules and regulations calculated to promote safety and efficiency of operations.[2]

---

[1] See also Bureau of Mines, Yearbook, 1916.

[2] "As to the relations of the Bureau of Mines to the work of the States and private corporations, it may be expected that the bureau will take no part in mine supervision or in mine inspection, these being within the province of the State. But the Bureau will do what it can to encourage the investigation of local mining problems by the States and the private corporations most directly interested. Furthermore, the bureau will not undertake to do or to supplant the professional work which is now being done, or is to be done, by private mining engineers. Its main work will

The activities of the bureau may be grouped roughly under the two following heads:

Safeguarding the lives of workers in the mineral industries, and developing more efficient and less wasteful methods for the mining, preparation, treatment, and utilization of mineral substances.

Promotion of Safety and Health. The Bureau of Mines is directly concerned with the safety and health of workers in mines of all kinds, in quarries, and in metallurgical establishments. It does not interest itself in the welfare of the individual worker, but in general conditions which affect the welfare of groups of workers. Its activities in this direction follow the lines of investigation and research, instruction, and training.

Investigation of Accidents. Investigations of mine accidents, begun by the Technologic Branch of the Geological Survey in 1907, have been conducted by the Bureau of Mines since its organization. Particular attention has been given to coal-mine explosions on account of their high record of fatalities, but as the service has developed, attention has been given to falls of roof, falls of coal, and accidents connected with the hoisting and hauling of coal. The investigative work includes accidents and the development of appliances and methods for their prevention in the coal-mining, metal-mining, quarrying, and metallurgical industries. After every investigation, a report is furnished to the mine operator, setting forth changes deemed advisable to insure greater safety.

Research in Accident Prevention. While recognizing the importance of investigating individual accidents, the bureau has placed increasing emphasis on researches to determine the

be that of conducting such investigations and inquiries as relate to the more general or national phases of the mining and metallurgical branches of the industry, and the distribution of the results of its investigations and inquiries among the mine workers and mine operators of the country in such manner as will be most effective in accomplishing the purposes for which the bureau was created."—Secretary of the Interior, Annual Report, 1919, p. 28.

ACTIVITIES

conditions that lead to accidents and how they may be removed or controlled. A beginning was made by the Technologic Branch of the Geological Survey in 1908, under the terms of an appropriation act which provided for studies of the causes of mine explosions.

In its first year of operation, the bureau leased a tract of coal land near Bruceton, Pennsylvania, and opened a small experimental mine for the study of coal-dust explosions. The plan as announced and carried through was the "driving of a double entry or tunnel, into the coal bed for about 2,000 feet and then opening from the entries, a few rooms in which experiments may be conducted to determine, under the conditions of actual mining, the behavior of different types of explosives, the conditions that determine the ignition of gas or dust, or mixture of gas or dust and air, and the factors involved in the spread of the resulting explosions." This mine is equipped with apparatus for recording the speed of an explosion and the pressure produced and for automatically taking samples of the gases formed during an explosion. The explosibility of the dusts of bituminous coals from different fields throughout the country has been demonstrated at this mine and methods of preventing or limiting explosions by the use of rock dust have been devised.

Frequent public demonstrations have been held in the presence of large gatherings of miners and mine officers.

Laboratory tests, both physical and chemical, are also regularly made of dusts, gases, and explosives. In the case of explosives used in coal mines, the bureau's initial efforts were productive of almost immediate results. Said the Annual Report for 1913:

At the time of the inauguration of this work black powder, with its long flame and poisonous gases, was almost universally used in coal-mining operations in the United States. One of the first investigations undertaken by the bureau was that looking to improvement in the character of the explosives used. As a result of conferences with mine owners, miners, and manufacturers of explosives, a number of these manufacturers agreed to undertake the making of a new type of explosive that would have for its special characteristics an explosion flame of short duration and relatively low temperature.

The bureau coöperated in the development of this new type of explosives by establishing the necessary standard with regard to safety, and by testing the explosives submitted from time to time to determine whether they had reached such standard, or the manner in which and the extent to which they failed to reach such standard. As a result of this work, within a little more than three years' time, the use of the new type of explosives, termed "permissible explosives," has become general in those mines where the risk of gas or dust explosions was a serious one.

Further conferences have been held in succeeding years, resulting in the development of other tests in further safeguarding the lives of miners.

From the first the bureau has given attention to the development of safer types of mine equipment and the promotion of their manufacture and installation. After examination of the equipment in common use, new or improved types were designed and constructed, and the coöperation of manufacturers was enlisted in the development and commercial production of those which had been perfected. New types submitted by manufacturers are subjected to test, and upon satisfactory performance they are formally "approved" and entered upon permissible lists.

As a result of the bureau's efforts in this direction, marked improvements have been effected in the types of portable electric mine lamps, explosion-proof motors, storage-battery locomotives, mine-lamp cords, flash lamps, flame safety lamps, gas detectors, danger signals, and coal-cutting apparatus. Studies of hoisting ropes, and safety catches for mine-hoisting cages, safety gates for mine shafts, and mine ladders have also been pursued. In coöperation with professional societies, operators, and equipment manufacturers, codes of rules setting standards of safety for the use of electricity underground, for the installation and operation of electrical equipment in bituminous coal mines and for metal mines, have been com-

ACTIVITIES

piled, and their adoption has been productive of better conditions. Several states have enacted stricter laws governing mine equipment; these laws being based upon recommendation of the Bureau of Mines.

No less important is the work in connection with mine-rescue apparatus, which has resulted in the improvement of breathing apparatus and gas masks and the perfection of danger signals and signal detectors. A recent study has been made of the geophone, to determine its value in mining work.

Investigation of Mine Hazards. The investigation of mine hazards is another important feature of the bureau's work. This involves a study of the layout of the mine and methods of mining, timbering, transportation, hoisting, and dumping, with special reference to safety of employees, also the methods of storage, handling, and the use of explosives, fire fighting equipment, and rescue apparatus, and generally of the conditions under which mining operations are conducted and the lessening of mining hazards. Similar field investigations have been made of the working conditions in quarries. The results of these studies are made available to the operators and to the mining interests generally.

Investigations have also been made as to the causes and prevention of accidents at blast furnaces.

Investigation of Hygenic Conditions. Matters of hygiene also come within the scope of activities of the bureau. The organic act creating the bureau states that the "Director shall prepare and publish reports of inquiries and investigations with appropriate recommendations concerning the nature, causes, and prevention of accidents and improvements of conditions, methods, and equipment with special reference to health .... in the mining, quarrying, metallurgical, and other mineral industries."

In 1912 a committee of surgeons, as consultants, investigated the various methods for resustication after asphyxia due to mine gases. This resulted in obtaining information indicating that the Schaefer Method was superior to other methods. About the same time, development of first-aid was begun, chiefly by consultants to the bureau. This work has been carried on by the regular personnel of the bureau until at the present time the methods have been practically standardized as far as the mining industry is concerned.

Special studies in mine camp sanitation and oil camp sanitation have been made and reports published with recommendations for improvements. Among the principal studies of health hazards has been that of carbon monoxide, including its physiological effects on both men and animals, together with methods for its determination and treatment. The problem of the ventilation of mines, including the effects of non-poisonous gases and the effects of temperatures and humidity, has been extensively investigated. The effects of coal dust have been and are to be investigated, but on a much smaller scale. The effects of various poisonous dusts, as mercury, lead, and arsenic, in the mines and smelters, have been and are also being investigated. Special reports have been written and forwarded to those most vitally interested.

During the past year a study has been made of medical organizations in mining communities with a view to making recommendations for their efficient operation. Health and safety campaigns are being successfully carried on in some of the districts by car engineers and car surgeons.

In the study of conditions favoring occupational diseases in the mining industries, the bureau has coöperated with the United States Public Health Service and with state organizations pursuing similar special investigations. Subjects which have been thus considered are: pulmonary disease among miners, hookworm, mine ventilation, health conditions in the quicksilver industry and in steel and metallurgical plants.

In its initial report the bureau recognized the danger of overlapping and duplication in this work, and in 1916 it declared that with respect to health conditions in steel and metallurgical plants "it seems only necessary for the Bureau of Mines to coöperate . . . in the matter of special technical

ACTIVITIES

questions that may come up from time to time."[3] In the sundry civil appropriation act for 1918 and succeeding years, Congress has provided that "the Secretary of the Treasury may detail medical officers of the Public Health Service for coöperative health, safety, or sanitary work with the Bureau of Mines." Under this authority, the medical personnel of the rescue cars and stations is detailed from the Public Health Service under a coöperative agreement.

Incident to its investigation of gases in mines as affecting the health of mine workers, the bureau in 1920 conducted a thorough investigation of automobile exhaust gases in vehicular tunnels, their composition, their production by different types of vehicles, and their removal through proper ventilation.

Operation of Mine-Rescue Stations and Cars. The purpose of the mine-rescue, or better, "mine-safety," stations and cars was set forth in the bureau's first annual report (1911):

Early in the investigation of mine disasters it was necessary to provide, in the important coal fields, facilities for enabling engineers to examine mines after disasters, while the mines were still full of poisonous explosive gases, in order that examination might be made while the evidences of a disaster were still fresh. It was found also that such prompt examinations would be useful in opening up these mines and in rescuing miners who might have been entombed. For the above reasons, there has been established in those of the larger coal fields in which mine disasters are most likely, mine-safety stations or mine-safety cars.

At that time there were six stations and six cars, the latter being second-hand Pullman cars refitted. The operation of these stations and cars was described in that report as follows:

These cars do not remain at their headquarters, but each within its own district moves from one mining camp to another. When a serious mine disaster occurs in any district

[3] Annual Report, 1916, p. 68.

the car in that district immediately drops its ordinary program and is carried to the scene of the disaster either by special locomotive or by the first available train. The men of the car, together with such local men as have had mine-rescue training, examine the mine as quickly as possible, penetrating the poisonous and explosive gases in it by means of the breathing apparatus that they wear, and aiding in the rescue of any persons who may have been entombed in the mine. In case of a disaster in the coal fields near one of the . . . stations . . . the miner in charge of the station, with all available rescue and first-aid equipment, proceeds by the first train to the scene of the disaster, and endeavors to accomplish, with the help of locally trained miners, the purposes mentioned above. . . .

The mining engineers of the bureau examine the safety conditions at mines, advise the mine officials as to the possibilities of improving these conditions, and deliver illustrated lectures to miners, calling their attention to the need of greater care in safeguarding their own lives and the lives of others. Daily demonstrations of mine-rescue and first-aid equipment and methods are given. Miners are trained in the practical methods of handling such equipment under mine-disaster conditions. . . .

Permanent results are appearing in the establishment of a considerable number of local rescue and first-aid stations equipped by mining companies and manned by experienced local mining engineers competent to investigate mine conditions, conduct safety demonstrations, and to advise mine officials and miners as to methods for preventing mine accidents. . . .

It is expected that ultimately the mine-rescue and first-aid work will be taken care of locally through the training and organization of miners at each of the larger mines or groups of mines in the different coal fields, and that this work will then be supported entirely by the coal-mining companies. The work undertaken by the Bureau of Mines is pioneer educational work, temporary in character.

By 1921 the number of stations had been increased to ten, and the number of cars to ten, of which six were new steel cars. Seven of the stations were equipped with auto rescue trucks. "This method of disseminating information," says one annual report, "is more effective than any other possible

ACTIVITIES

system. Its advantages over publications will be appreciated by those who understand that a majority of these miners are foreign born and ordinarily read little or no English printed matter."

Persons who receive certificates of first-aid training are instructed and examined in the anatomy of the human body, the treatment of hemorrhage, fractures, burns, and shock, and the transport of wounded persons. Certificates of rescue training are given persons who pass a physical examination for fitness for rescue work, wear breathing apparatus while doing hard labor in atmospheres containing noxious or irrespirable gases, and demonstrate their ability to adjust and take care of such apparatus, and to perform the duties of rescue men. The training given represents fifteen hours of intensive work.

During the decade ending June 30, 1920, the Bureau of Mines trained 50,971 persons in rescue and first-aid methods. Of this number 30,333 persons received first-aid training only, 4836 received mine-rescue training only, and 15,802 were trained both in mine-rescue and first-aid work.

The number trained (734) in 1911 represented less than one miner in every thousand employed. In 1920, the number trained was 8993, which, based upon the estimated total number of mine employees for that year, represented about nine in every thousand. The total number of persons trained during the entire ten-year period indicates that for every thousand employees at coal and metal mines approximately fifty-five have received training in rescue or first-aid work, or both, from the Bureau of Mines.

Publicity. As a means of stimulating public interest in first-aid and rescue work, the Bureau of Mines has encouraged the holding of mine-rescue and first-aid contests and field meets throughout the mining regions.

The results of the bureau's researches and investigations in mine safety are published as "Bulletins" and "Technical Papers" or in the form of "Miners' Circulars," the latter being written in simple, non-technical English and widely distributed among workers in mines, quarries, and metallurgical plants.

Since its establishment the bureau has regularly compiled and published reports on mine fatalities in order to provide a body of reliable information for use in determining the hazards of workmen in the mineral industries and the steps to be taken in lessening the death rate from accidents. Information as to accidents in coal mines is furnished by the various state mine inspectors, and the returns are issued monthly. Accidents in metal mines, quarries, coke ovens, and metallurgical plants, except blast-furnaces, are reported voluntarily by the operators, and the returns are published annually.

Technological Researches and Investigations. The technologic work of the Bureau of Mines, extending as it does through the various mining and metallurgical industries, is of such a varied nature as almost to defy classification. In the following paragraphs it is considered under a series of heads which are accurately descriptive but not mutually exclusive.

Mining. Studies of mining methods, and equipment with respect to safety and efficiency have been continuously conducted, and unsafe and wasteful methods called to the attention of the mine operators. Many of the investigations relative to methods and equipment for lessening mine hazards have already been described under Research in Accident Prevention. The testing and development of safer types of explosives, the explosibility tests of mine gases and dusts, and the perfecting of stone-dust barriers and other means for preventing or limiting explosions in coal mines, have added greatly to safety from explosion hazards. A country-wide study is being made of mine-explosion hazards and mine-fire hazards. After each explosion or fire, a careful investigation is made with a view to ascertaining the probable origin, the effects, and what can be done to lessen the likelihood of a similar disaster in the same or other mines.

ACTIVITIES

Besides assistance rendered by the crews of the rescue cars and stations at disasters, bureau engineers frequently assist or direct the work of fighting mine fires. A special technique has been developed by which a mine fire may be more readily brought under control and the extent of the danger area determined by improved gas analysis devices and other means.

Methods of timbering and other means of support have been studied both with regard to safety of the workers and from the viewpoint of the practical mining man. Attention is also being given to methods for the preservation of mine timbers. Studies of mine explosives and blasting methods are made with regard to economy as well as safety. They include the use of various explosives new in mining; for example, liquid oxygen explosive, and excess stocks of military explosives released for industrial use. With a view to lessening waste and finding cheaper and better methods in the handling of coal or ore and waste, in underground mines, the bureau investigates methods for the separation of impurities from the coal (or ore) in the mines, disposal of the waste, and the loading and transportation of ore and waste.

Experiments are conducted in methods of coal washing and preparation, and coal washing practice is studied with a view to reduction of losses of good coal and widening the field of use of the more impure coals.

Special studies have been made in zinc mining and treatment with a view to reducing waste in the zinc mines of Wisconsin, Oklahoma, Missouri, Kansas, and other states. Comprehensive mining investigations have included studies of methods employed in the iron-mining industry, placer mining, open-pit copper mining, and the operation of gold dredges. Information is being collected for a monograph on coal mining practice in the United States with a view to affording comparison of the methods employed in different fields and making information on the more efficient practices available to all.

Tunnel methods and equipment, from the point of view of

both safety and efficiency, have been made the subject of investigation and report; also the corrosion of metals in mine equipment. To aid operators of mines to obtain the economies practicable through careful accounting, descriptions of mine accounting systems have been prepared and published.

The bureau, in the first year of its existence, made a preliminary examination into quarry methods and practices, having in mind the reduction of risk to life, efficiency of operation, and the elimination and utilization of quarry waste. In 1914, in coöperation with the Geological Survey and the Bureau of Standards, an extensive investigation was made of building-stone quarries. This included a study of marble and sandstone quarry methods in 1914 and 1915, and in the next two years, studies of methods of quarrying limestone for Portland cement and for blast-furnace flux. During 1920 and 1921, a detailed study of slate quarrying was conducted, having in view improved methods of operation and utilization of waste.

As the mining industry is world-wide in its extent and as progress is being made on its problems in other countries, the Bureau of Mines has recognized the importance of collecting from all sources information as to all phases of the subject for the guidance of the agencies of the national and state governments as well as those whose interest lies either in pure science or in its practical application. This involves an examination of mines by field engineers, and of the literature of the subject as presented in books, in the papers of scientific societies, and in periodicals.

In 1919 a comprehensive glossary of all known terms used in the mining and mineral industry by English-speaking people was published.

In 1912 the Chief Mining Engineer headed a party of mining engineers on a three-months' trip through the mines of several countries of Europe with a view to bringing about "the adoption in American mining operations of any practices that elsewhere have proved effective in reducing the loss

ACTIVITIES 19

of life or the waste of resources and seem applicable to American conditions." Again in 1919 the Chief Mining Engineer visited the United Kingdom, Belgium, France, and Germany, to observe and report on mining methods.

Through district mining engineers stationed and working in the various mining districts of the United States, a constant interchange of information takes place as to improved methods and practices. Much of this work does not lend itself to formal publication, but to be effective must be imparted to those engaged in the industry by personal contact under mining conditions and in the mines themselves. Thus continual advice is given to promote greater recovery of coal and mineral, to improve ventilation underground, and to further the introduction of safe practices, and demonstrations are made under working conditions of the use of explosives and a variety of improved mine equipment.

Studies of rock dust in relation to pulmonary disease among metal miners in certain mining districts have demonstrated the need for more adequate protection of metal mine workers. A general investigation of metal mines is in progress covering ventilation, rock dust, and temperatures and humidities in metal mine workings, in respect to their relation, one to another, and their effect on the health, comfort, and efficiency of the workers.

The bureau under authority conferred by the Secretary of the Interior, has coöperated with the Indian Office in supervising mining methods in mines on Indian lands, and makes recommendations for the increase of safety and prevention of waste in mining coal and other minerals. The bureau has also coöperated in appraising the coal under lands belonging to Indian tribes, and assists the Indian Office by giving technical advice and making reports in connection with the leasing of coal lands, oil lands, and (Act of June 30, 1919; 41 Stat., L., 3) with metalliferous minerals on Indian lands.

The mining engineers coöperate with national or state legal bodies and societies or organizations interested in promoting safety and efficiency in mining, by contributing technical advice in the revision of mining codes, and lend their support in putting improved codes into effect.

Mineral Technology. In the field of miscellaneous mineral technology the bureau has concerned itself with the increase of efficiency in the utilization of mineral substances and especially with reducing the dependence of American industry upon foreign sources. Attention has been directed to deposits of fuller's earth, feldspar, kaolin, and clays available to centers of consumption. In 1917 an experiment station was established at Columbus, to deal exclusively with problems of ceramics. Information of value to the talc and soapstone industries is now being collected.

After the outbreak of the war in Europe, the matter of industrial self-sufficiency took on increased importance, and upon the entrance of the United States in 1917, the military motive became paramount. In coöperation with the War Department, the bureau conducted investigations of the nitrate situation and of the processes used in fixing atmospheric nitrogen. In coöperation with the Council of National Defense, the bureau studied the problem of mineral raw materials for sulphuric acid manufacture. Attention was also given to developing domestic sources of graphite suitable for making crucibles and of potash for fertilizer, explosives, and other uses.

An important series of special investigations relates to the extraction of rare metals for native ores.

Particular attention has been given to the production of radium for use in the treatment of cancer. The situation at the outset was thus described in an annual report of the bureau (1913):

There is probably not more than 30 grams (about 1 ounce) of radium now available for such treatment in all countries. Of this amount there is probably not more than 2 grams of radium bromide in the United States, in the hands of a few surgeons. Probably 15 grams of radium bromide was produced during 1912; and of this 15 grams nearly 11.5 grams was extracted in various European countries from ores shipped to them from the United States—mainly from Colorado and Utah. . . .

Meanwhile the American hospitals are vainly endeavoring to purchase and bring back to the United States for their own use some small part of this radium, even at such prices as $120,000 to $160,000 per gram, or $500,000 to $800,000 for the 5 grams of radium that a large hospital should have or have access to for special cases. . . .

Owing to the lack of funds with which to carry on the work, the Bureau of Mines made a coöperative agreement with the National Radium Institute for the purpose of studying the best methods of handling carnotite ore and of producing therefrom radium, uranium, and vanadium. An experimental plant was established at Denver by the Institute and placed under the supervision of investigators in the bureau service. This plant was soon enlarged to a commercial size, and by the end of the coöperative arrangement in 1917 it had produced eight and a half grams of radium element in the form of radium bromide, at a cost of only $40,000 per gram. The processes of extracting radium that were developed were patented for the benefit of the people of the United States.

Metallurgy. An investigation of smelter fumes was undertaken in California, with the idea of preventing damage to national forests. This work was extended to the recovery and utilization of valuable substances in the fumes. Smelter and refining plants in different parts of the country were examined and laboratory tests made. The Director of the Bureau of Mines served on two commissions concerned with smelter smoke problems in California and Montana, and the bureau coöperated with private companies in similar investigations. Attention has also been given to the prevention of injury to animals and vegetation by the solution discharged from cyanide plants.

As funds became available other metallurgical work was undertaken, the principal object of which was the prevention of waste, the recovery of losses in metals, and the commercial utilization of unworked mineral deposits.

An idea of the general range of the metallurgical activities of the bureau can be best conveyed through enumeration of the subjects of representative investigations. They include hydrometallurgy of gold and silver; cyanidation of silver ores; measurement of blast-furnace slag viscosity; melting of brass and of aluminum chips; treatment of various low-grade and complex ores, especially lead, zinc, silver, and iron; recovery of silver from oxidized ores; the flotation process for lead and zinc ores; recovery of mercury; the volatilization process for lead and silver ores; recovery of potash at cement plants and blast furnaces; metals needed in the preparation of special alloy steels; melting of non-ferrous alloys; and preparation of luminous metallic paint.

Incidental to the production of radium, many tons of iron vanadate applicable to the production of high-grade vanadium steel and many tons of oxide of uranium for use in coloring glass and hardening tool-steel were produced. The extracting of molybdenum, tungsten, manganese, pyrite, and nickel from native ores was the subject of investigation before the entrance of the United States into the World War, the purpose being to develop larger domestic supplies of those minerals necessary to the industries of the United States.

After the United States went into the war this work took on increased importance, and its scope was greatly widened to include mercury, chromium, antimony, arsenic, platinum, and tin. Under special authorization of Congress (Act of October 5, 1918; 40 Stat. L., 1009) the bureau was planning to extend its investigations relating to minerals of military importance, when the signing of the armistice put an end to the work.

Solid Mineral Fuels. A knowledge of the chemical and physical nature of the substances constituting coal is an important aid in attaining efficiency in the utilization of coal and in understanding the behavior of different coals in burning.

Also such knowledge is of especial value in considering the causes of dust explosions in mines and mills, and in determining why some coals coke and other do not. From the first the bureau has conducted investigations into the origin and constitution of coal, including chemical studies, microscopic studies, and studies of the decomposition of coal and the primary products and by-products thereof.

To determine the possible utilization of the low-grade fuel resources of the country the bureau has also conducted a series of investigations of lignite and peat from the point of view of both direct burning and the extraction of valuable constituents. Provision for this work was made in the original organic act and in subsequent acts of appropriation. In 1919 a special act (Act of February 25, 1919; 40 Stat. L., 1154) granted the sum of $100,000 for further studies.

In 1920 a special study was made of conditions in the coal industry, particularly as regards the standardization of coal for export.

Fuel-efficiency tests, begun by the Geological Survey, have been continued and widened in scope by the Bureau of Mines. The conditions under which different types of fuel can be burned with greatest efficiency have been studied and the best type for particular uses determined. Representative investigations which may be cited are: The combustion process in a fuel bed; clinkering tendency of coal; briquetting of low-grade coal and lignite; use of powdered coal; and use of coal and coke in domestic furnaces. Attention has also been given to efficient methods of firing, air supply, developing means for the abatement of the smoke nuisance in cities, and efficiency testing of boilers with various fuels. Furnace design has been considered with reference to complete combustion of the various fuels to be used; tests have been made of different types of furnaces and boilers; and gas producers have been studied with a view to better utilization of fuel. Other allied subjects investigated are: Heat transmission into boilers; heat insulation of furnaces; and boiler and furnace efficiency in government heating and power plants. Work of this nature for other branches of the government has been continuous and extensive. Particular attention has been given to coke; its use in foundry practice and its valuable by-products.

Several branches of the national government which store large quantities of coal have called upon the bureau for investigations of the risk of spontaneous combustion of coal stored under different conditions and also of the loss of heating values through deterioration during storage in the open air or under water. The results of a five-year study were made available in 1917 and 1918.

From the Geological Survey was transferred one of the most important of the bureau's activies; namely, the testing and analysis of coals, lignite, and other mineral fuels purchased under specification for the use of the government, to ascertain whether those fuels conform to the contract stipulations under which they were purchased. This involves sampling, laboratory tests and analysis, and steaming tests. The direct results have been a saving in government fuel outlays and a more adequate set of specifications. Many cities and a number of states as well as private corporations have followed the plans adopted by the national government in their purchases of fuel.

The investigation of coals, lignite, and other mineral fuels belonging to the United States and the manner in which they can be developed and used to best advantage and with least waste is another activity inherited from the Geological Survey and broadened and extended by the bureau. This involves the collection of samples, in coöperation with the Geological Survey, and elaborate chemical and physical analyses and tests. In 1913 the Director of the bureau exercised general supervision over an expedition to the Matanuska coal field in Alaska to determine whether the coal was suitable for navy use; and in 1918 an engineer in the service of the bureau was detailed by the Secretary of the Interior as a member of a party to investigate and report on the development of the coal beds in that field.

In 1920-21 an engineer from the bureau served on the engineering staff of the Super Power Survey.

Petroleum and Natural Gas. From its inception, the bureau has recognized the importance of exact knowledge as to the nature of petroleum and natural gas, and has carried out investigations into the character of the various petroleums found throughout the United States and the products made from them. It has done this with a view to determining their value and chemical composition and the methods of utilizing them efficiently as power producers in industrial plants, on ships, for motor vehicles, and as lubricants. These investigations cover the heavier distillates of petroleum as well as of kerosene and gasoline. Studies have been made of the natural gas of the oil fields, and special attention given to the possibility of recovering gasoline and their products on a commercial scale from natural gas ordinarily wasted or inefficiently used. Attention has also been given to the possible loss in the heating value of natural gas through the removal of gasoline.

The prevention of waste of petroleum and natural gas has been the chief motive underlying the bureau's studies of production, storage, and distribution, although the lessening of the danger to human life has not been overlooked. These investigations have had to do with such matters as types of derricks, tools, and appliances used in well-drilling, underground engineering problems, the cementation process for excluding water, the use of mud-laden fluid in drilling operations to eliminate the waste of gas and oil, the capping of "gushers" and "gassers," the handling of producing wells, the use of water or compressed air to recover oil that can not be recovered by the usual pumping methods, the separation of gas and oil from flowing wells by means of gas traps, the gaging of oil walls, and the boring and operation of oil and gas wells through workable coal beds. The Bureau of Mines had also carried out many investigations in the field and has worked with operators in California, Kansas, Oklahoma, Texas, Louisiana, Wyoming, Illinois, and West Virginia in overcoming local operating problems and demonstrating methods of conservation.

In 1920 the Secretary of the Interior appointed the Director of the bureau chairman of a committee to make a study of the natural gas situation throughout the United States, and to formulate recommendations for conserving the supply. The importance of this work is indicated by the fact that the bureau's investigations have shown that the annual waste of petroleum and natural gas amounts to billions of dollars.

Included in this figure are the losses of great magnitude in the storage of petroleum and petroleum products through seepage, bottom sediments, evaporation, and fire. Studies have therefore been made of storage methods, and designs for improved reservoirs and tanks have been prepared. Fires at oil wells and tanks have been investigated and better methods of prevention and extinguishing proposed. Problems dealing with the transportation of oil both by railroad and by pipe line have been solved.

As an aid to oil operators the bureau has made a detailed study of the decline and ultimate production of oil properties, thereby providing the means for appraising oil properties and estimating the oil that may be obtained from prospective oil properties or from producing oil properties. As a further aid it has made available the result of a study of cost accounts for oil producers.

For the Bureau of Internal Revenue, the Bureau of Mines has developed new principles and methods of evaluating oil and gas lands for taxation. These methods have been generally adopted. For the Secretary of the Interior, it has made a special study of the value of the natural gas in various fields, and prepared operating regulations for oil and gas wells on government-leased land under the Leasing Act of February 21, 1920 (41 Stat. L., 437, 441).

ACTIVITIES

Refinery practice also comes within the scope of the bureau's activities. To facilitate this work, coöperative relations were established with a large number of scientific societies, and an experimental refinery has been constructed and is in operation. Particular attention has been given to the extraction of gasoline from petroleum, natural gas, and oil-bearing shales. One result of this work was the development of a new process for the production of gasoline, benzene, and toluene from petroleum. Special methods for treating benzene and toluol for use in the dye and explosive industries have also been devised.

A related investigation is concerned with the recovery of oils and various by-products therefrom from oil shales found in great abundance in Utah, Colorado, and Wyoming. In addition to studies of the quality and the yields of oil and by-products from various oil shales of the United States, complete laboratory investigations of these products have been made. Work to determine what refining processes will be most satisfactory for American shales is being carried on, and prospective operators are advised from time to time as to the actual status of the American oil-shale industry.

Since 1918 the bureau has collected statistics showing the amount of oil run to the stills, the refineries throughout the United States, and the output and stocks of refined products, such as gasoline, kerosene, lubricants, fuel oil and miscellaneous oils. These figures are published monthly.

Since 1915 the bureau has prepared a series of bibliographies on petroleum and allied substances, with a view to presenting annually references to books, official reports, and important articles in periodicals. These are issued monthly in mimeographed form and printed annually as bulletins.

Reference has been made to the testing and analysis of fuels for government use that is currently performed by the Bureau of Mines. Among these fuels are included petroleum and petroleum products. As early as 1911 the bureau prepared and recommended for adoption, desirable specifications for petroleum products, and suggested efficient methods of testing and utilization. In 1918 an Executive Order authorized the establishment of a committee on the standardization of specifications for petroleum products. This committee, on which the bureau was represented, adopted the specifications for petroleum products now used by the government. Field examinations have been made and technical and practical advice has been given to other government bureaus in connection with the operations of various oil properties on public lands. In 1915 the Bureau of Mines began a series of surveys of motor gasoline marketed in the United States, and such surveys are now made twice a year.

For the use of its engineers in connection with their petroleum and natural gas investigations, the bureau has prepared detail drawings covering oil and gas fields and the location of wells, storage tanks, and pipe lines.

Upon the entrance of the United States into the World War the activities of the bureau in relation to petroleum became more intense and varied. In coöperation with the Geological Survey a report was prepared in 1917 on the general conditions in the petroleum industry, to show whether war needs could be readily met. An educational campaign was undertaken to eliminate waste in the use of gasoline. Specifications for the gasoline to be used for aeroplanes were prepared and the grades of gasoline best adapted for different types of aeroplane motors were determined. Fuel submitted for use in aeroplane motors was tested. Technical advice was given on the boring of test wells in England, and experts were released from the bureau's service to superintend the work of drilling. Petroleum engineers were also sent overseas to serve on the Inter-Allied Petroleum Conference of the Allied Maritime Transport Council, dealing with supplies, stocks, specifications, storage, transportation, and allocation of petroleum products for the allied countries and the American Expeditionary Forces. In the course of this work active coöperation was maintained with the Fuel Administration, the Shipping Board, and the military branches of the government. At the cessation of active hostilities, therefore, the bureau was confronted with many additional problems that had arisen during the war, which were pressing for solution. With increased appropriations and facilities the Bureau of Mines is now studying every branch of the petroleum industry from time drilling starts to the time the products are consumed.

Coöperation. Since the mining and metallurgical industries are country-wide in extent and varied in nature and in methods of control, the Bureau of Mines has entered into many cooperative agreements for the conduct of work within its field. These have included other branches of the national government, many state and local governments. educational institutions, scientific societies, and private agencies wishing to pursue a basic investigation of importance to the whole industry. It brings into this coöperative work, the viewpoint of the engineer and metallurgist.

In 1920 the bureau had formal coöperative agreements with state agencies in eleven states, twelve universities, and nineteen private and semiprivate agencies. The total amount of money spent by these outside agencies on coöperative work was about $500,000 during the fiscal year 1919-20. The terms of the agreements necessarily vary with individual cases. The manner in which they are arranged is as follows:

Some State, or university, private or semiprivate organization has problems in mining or metallurgy the solution of which would benefit itself and the public.

These outside agencies agree to pay part or all of the cost, both in personnel and materials, of the investigation, which is to be carried on under the direction of and according to the methods of the Bureau of Mines.

The Bureau of Mines retains the right to make public and print the results of all such investigations.

Congress in 1920 (Act of June 5, 1920; 41 Stat. L., 874, 913) provided that during the fiscal year 1920-21 branches of the national government having funds available for scientific investigations within the scope of the functions of the Bureau of Mines which that bureau was unable to perform within the limits of its appropriations, with the approval of the Secretary of the Interior, might transfer to the Bureau of Mines such sums as might be necessary to carry on the work.

Formal coöperative agreements with state agencies effective in 1920 are listed as below:

University of Arizona,—Improvement of conditions in the mining, quarrying, metallurgical, and miscellaneous mineral industries, with special reference to the treatment of low-grade copper ores.

Industrial Accident Commission of California,—Improvement of conditions in mining, quarrying, metallurgical, and other mineral industries, safeguarding life among employees, and preventing unnecessary waste of resources.

University of California,—Improvement of conditions in mining, quarrying, metallurgical, and other mineral industries, with special reference to quicksilver and the precious metals.

University of Idaho, and the Idaho Bureau of Mines and Geology,—Improvement of conditions in the mining, quarrying, metallurgical, and other mineral industries, with special reference to the losses that take place in the mining and milling of lead and zinc ores, safeguarding life among employees, and preventing unnecessary waste of resources.

Colorado School of Mines,—Recovery of values from rare metals and from low-grade and complex ores.

Engineering Experiment Station of the University of Illinois, and Illinois Geological Survey,—Coal-mining methods, means of promoting the safety of coal miners, and methods of utilizing coal.

University of Minnesota,—Improvement of conditions in the mining, quarrying, metallurgical, and other mineral industries, especially in connection with the mining and concentration of iron and manganese ores, safeguarding life among employees and preventing unnecessary waste of resources.

New York Bridge and Tunnel Commission and the New Jersey Interstate Bridge and Tunnel Commission,—Investigations with reference to exhaust gases of motor vehicles and the physiological effects of carbon monoxide gas.

State of Oklahoma,—Improvement of conditions in the oil

industry by safeguarding life among employees and preventing unnecessary waste of resources.

Ohio State University,—Increased efficiency in the utilization of mineral substances necessary to the ceramic industry, stimulating and upbuilding this industry and substituting ceramic products of American manufacture for those now imported.

Oregon Bureau of Mines and Geology,—Improvement of conditions in the mining, quarrying, metallurgical, and other mineral industries, safeguarding life among employees, and preventing unnecessary waste of resources.

Industrial Commission of the State of Utah,—Methods of mining that relate to health, sanitation, and safety conditions, and the appliances best adapted to prevent accidents in mines, mills, and smelters; the improvement of conditions affecting health and safety in mining, milling, and smelting; improvements in the use of explosives and electricity in such operations; inquiries and investigations relating to health, sanitation, and safety in the mining and metallurgical industries, and the obtaining of prompt and reliable reports of accidents to persons in such industries.

State School of Mines of the University of Utah,—Recovery of valuable mineral from low-grade and complex ores, the prevention of waste and the increase of efficiency in the preparation, treatment, and utilization of mineral substances.

University of Washington,—Improvement of conditions in the mining, quarrying, metallurgical and other mineral industries, with special reference to mining and preparation of coals, dressing of low-grade ores, and electro-metallurgy; safeguarding life among employees, and preventing unnecessary waste of resources.

Administration. Although the Bureau of Mines is essentially an agency of investigation and research, certain administrative duties have been imposed upon it which merit attention in any summary consideration of its activities.

Inspection of Mines and Mine Leases. By direction of the Secretary of the Interior and by virtue of the act of March 3, 1891 (26 Stat. L., 1104) mine inspection in the territories was placed in 1910 under the supervision of the Director of the Bureau of Mines. The mine inspector for Alaska, reports through the Director of the Bureau of Mines to the Secretary of the Interior. His duties are necessarily varied in character, but special attention is paid to mining practice with reference to safety.

In 1913, by direction of the Secretary, the bureau was made responsible for the inspection of coal-mine leases on the public lands, and also for the inspection of coal, asphalt, and other mines and of the oil and gas wells on lands belonging to the Indians, the latter being in coöperation with the Office of Indian Affairs.

Mineral Land Leases. In 1916 the bureau coöperated with the other bureaus of the Department of the Interior in carrying out the provisions of an act of Congress (Act of October 20, 1914; 38 Stat. L., 741) governing the leasing of coal lands in Alaska, the function of the bureau representatives being to recommend the proper division of the land into leasing units, and to assist in the preparation of regulations to control such leases.

The Bureau of Mines prepared operating regulations to govern the production of oil and gas on leased lands under the provision of the Leasing Act of February 25, 1920 (41 Stat. L., 437) and in November, 1920, the Secretary of the Interior put the bureau in immediate charge of the administration of these regulations.

Through the Chief Petroleum Technologist, the Oil and Gas Supervisor, and his assistants, the bureau supervises the drilling of wells and the production of oil and gas on public lands covered by this act, and in addition gages all oil and computes royalties due the government. Although this work has only begun, it is estimated that the Government's royalty during the first year will amount to over six million dollars. Public lands subject to the leasing act are located in at least fourteen states and in Alaska. To care for this work there is an organization of twenty-five petroleum engineers, expert drillers, gagers, and clerks. The office of the Chief Oil Supervisor is in Denver, and there are district offices at Caspar

ACTIVITIES 33

(Wyo.), Winnett (Mont.), Bakersfield (Calif.), and Shrevesport (La.). Recently the inspection and oversight of the operations on the Naval Reserve Oil Lands in California has been turned over to the Bureau of Mines.

On April 30, 1921, the Secretary of the Interior approved operating regulations, prepared by the bureau, to govern coal-mining methods and the safety and health of miners on leased lands, and charged the bureau with the duty of administering the regulations.

Supervision of mining operations, involving coal, phosphate, oil shale, and sodium is for the present conducted through a District Mining Supervisor, with an office in Denver, under the direction of the Chief Mining Engineer.

Explosives Regulation. In 1917 Congress passed the Explosives Regulation Act (Act of October 6, 1917; 40 Stat. L., 388) to govern the manufacture, distribution, storage, use or possession of explosives and their ingredients, the purpose being to protect the citizens and industries of the country from the careless or malicious use of explosives. Under this act, the Director of the Bureau of Mines was authorized to issue and revoke licenses for importers, exporters, manufacturers, dealers in and users of explosives, and generally to direct the administrative organization set up for the purpose of control, and, subject to the approval of the Secretary of the Interior, to frame the necessary rules and regulations. He was also authorized to investigate all explosions and fires in places in which explosive substances were made, stored, transported, or used, and in case of evidence of wilful act to take appropriate action. This act was declared to be effective "when the United States is at war," but following the armistice the licence requirements were relaxed with the idea of relieving normal industry from restrictions no longer necessary; and under a joint resolution approved March 3, 1921 (41 Stat. L., 1359), this act terminated.

Utilization of Surplus War Department Explosives. Upon representations of the Secretary of the Interior following tests made by the Bureau of Mines to determine the suitability of the explosives for engineering work, the War Department in 1918 turned over to the Department of the Interior about 30,000,000 pounds of trinitrotoluol ("T N T") and other explosives to be used on construction work of the national government. The Secretary of the Interior delegated to the Director of the Bureau, the supervision of the apportionment of these explosives among the several branches of the government.

By an amendment (Act of July 1, 1918; 40 Stat. L., 671) to the Explosives Regulation Act, the Director of the Bureau, under rules and regulations approved by the Secretary of the Interior, was authorized, during the period of the war, to limit by license the sale, possession, and use of platinum, palladium, and iridium and compounds thereof, because of the need of these metals in the equipment of plants manufacturing chemicals used in the production of explosives. Following the armistice, restrictions were removed.

War Minerals Relief. By an amendment (Act of March 2, 1919; 40 Stat. L., 1273) to the War Minerals Control Act of October 3, 1918, the Secretary of the Interior was authorized to examine claims and pay off financial losses of the producers of manganese, chrome, pyrite, and tungsten, where it could be shown that the production had taken place as a result of government action. Under this act a War Minerals Relief Commission was appointed, and the Director of the Bureau of Mines was authorized to appoint engineers and other force to conduct field engineering and accounting investigations needed for proper adjudication of the various claims, and also the office routine and administrative work of the commission.

There were filed under this act 1284 claims, of which seventy-seven were delinquent, having been filed subsequent to June 2, 1919.

Operation of the Government Fuel Yard. In 1918 Congress authorized the establishment of a Government Fuel Yard in the District of Columbia, and the purchase of all coal for plants of the national and district governments in and near the District, except the Navy Yard (Act of July 1, 1918; 40 Stat. L., 634,672). The establishment, maintenance, and operation of this yard was placed by the Secretary of the Interior under the direction of the Bureau of Mines, and a revolving fund was provided by Congress for the financing of the enterprise. About 275,000 tons are purchased and distributed each year.[4]

Compilation of Mining Laws and Regulations. The law examining work of the bureau has two main purposes: to assemble and review the laws and regulations most effective in increasing health, safety, and efficiency in mining, quarrying, and metallurgical establishments and to facilitate reasonable uniformity in legislation in the several states. To this end compilations have been made of the mining laws of the United States, the individual states, and foreign countries. Annotations are supplied setting forth judicial interpretations and decisions, and the rulings of administrative authorities. Separate digests have been prepared of the decisions of courts of record, of the General Land Office, and of all public officers showing the construction placed upon the substantive laws. In 1913 the first of a series of bulletins of abstracts of current decisions was issued. In 1915 a two-volume compilation of United States mining statutes from 1785 to 1914 was published. Supplementing this work is a series of bulletins of the annotated statutes of the separate states, the first of which, relating to California, was issued in 1918. In 1920 a compilation was made of the state laws governing the use of electricity in mines. In 1921 a compilation was made of the petroleum laws of the several states of the United States and of the other countries of North and South America.

War Activities. As soon as the entrance of the United States into the war seemed inevitable, the Bureau of Mines

[4] See Senate Select Committee on Reconstruction and Production, Hearings, p. 2063-80 (1921).
[5] See also War Work of the Bureau of Mines, Bulletin 178.

sought to render such special services in the emergency as were within the scope of its equipment and personnel. In order to enable the government to make the best use of the country's technical experts, the bureau at the request of the Council of National Defense coöperated in taking a census of chemists, metallurgists, and mining engineers. By reason of its experience in investigating deadly mine gases and the methods of protecting miners from them, the bureau in February, 1917, began a study of gas masks and rescue apparatus for military and naval purposes. This work, quickly supplemented by the study of war gases and smokes and methods of manufacturing them, led to the establishment of a special experiment station and the enrollment of a research staff of more than 700 chemists. All the work for the Army and Navy at this experiment station was in direct charge of the Bureau of Mines until July 1, 1918, when its control was transferred to the War Department by order of the President.

In coöperation with the War and Navy Departments, investigation was made of helium as a non-inflammable lifting gas for balloons, and a commercial plant for recovering helium from natural gas was designed, constructed, and placed in operation, under the supervision of the bureau's chemists. Work is now under way on perfecting mechanical details for maximum recovery and purity, studying the properties of gases at low temperature with special reference to separation of helium from natural gas, and on methods for storing helium in large quantites for future use. A study was made of methods of fixating atmospheric nitrogen and of oxidizing ammonia in order to manufacture nitrates needed in agriculture and for explosives, and the design of apparatus and plants for the oxidation of ammonia; and special investigations were made of minerals and metals needed in the production of military supplies. The bureau coöperated in the preparation and editing of a series of papers on the political and commercial control of minerals, these papers being compiled for use by the economic advisers of the American delegation to the Peace Conference.

CHAPTER III

ORGANIZATION

The Bureau of Mines is under the supervision of a Director who is appointed by the President subject to confirmation by the Senate. The Director is directly responsible to the Secretary of the Interior. Under the organic act he must be "thoroughly equipped for the duties of said office by technical education and experience." His salary is $6000, fixed by statute. The organic act provides also for a subordinate personnel, namely, "such experts and other employes, to be appointed by the Secretary of the Interior, as may be required to carry out the purposes of this act in accordance with the appropriations made from time to time by Congress for such purposes." It further provides a general limitation: that "in conducting inquiries and investigations authorized by this act neither the Director nor any member of the Bureau of Mines shall have any personal or private interest in any mine or the products of any mine under investigation, or shall accept employment from any private party for services in the examination of any mine or private mineral property, or issue any report as to the valuation or the management of any mine or other private mineral property"; but this is qualified by the authorization to employ temporarily, at a maximum per diem compensation of ten dollars, "in a consulting capacity or in the investigation of special subjects, any engineer or other expert whose principal professional practice is outside of such employment."

On August 15, 1921, there were 786 employees on duty, of whom 532 were in the "classified service."[1]

The bureau was reorganized on August 1, 1919, according

[1] List of positions, salary rates, and personnel appears in Appendix 1.

to the principles set forth in the following paragraphs from the Director's general order of that date:

The work intrusted to the Bureau involves matters both of business and of investigation. This necessitates that there shall be both administrative and technical control. In some matters, there is necessity for only the minimum of technical control since the work is either non-technical in character or follows established routine. In matters primarily investigative, it is desirable that the minimum of non-technical administrative control be exercised. For this reason the investigative work is set off as much as possible from the other work of the Bureau. The Bureau will, therefore, be organized with Investigations and Operations Branches with suitable subordinate divisions and sections, and so far as possible, work and personnel will be assigned to one or the other. It will be necessary in certain instances that the work be coöperative as between sections, divisions, or branches, or that a member of the Bureau may work for a period or regularly for part time with more than one section or division. In all cases the officers of the Bureau are charged with the duty of marking out a clear line of responsibility in regard both to administration and technical control, subject to the authority and final approval of the Director. Allotments and transfers of funds will be made for the various divisions of the work only on authority of the Director.

It is recognized, further that the character of and personnel engaged in investigation and research work is constantly changing. Problems are finished and new problems often inviting new policies and direction, are constantly being entered into. An investigation undertaken in one division or with a particular object in view may develop to be of major interest in some other division or field of the industry.

There are, therefore, the following three departments of the bureau's work:

    General Administration
    Operations Branch
    Investigations Branch

To insure coöperation throughout the bureau, each division has an advisory committee representing related services within the bureau organization.

ORGANIZATION

General Administration. Administrative work of a general nature is conducted through the following units:
> Office Proper of the Director
> Office of the Assistant Director
> Office of the Assistant to the Director

Office Proper of the Director. At the head of the service is the Director, who exercises general control over and coördinates the work of investigation and research. In the case of technical work not specifically assigned, the Director exercises immediate supervision.

Office of the Assistant Director. The position of Assistant Director was created in 1913 to handle such features of the administrative work as the Director might assign. Under the new organization the Assistant Director is in immediate charge of the Investigations Branch, and responsible to the Director for the final selection of problems, determination of the scope of investigations, choice of methods of study, inspection of work in progress, and criticism of results. Subject to appeal to the Director, he has veto power over the choice of personnel engaged on scientific or technical duties and the assignment of problems by superintendents of mining experiment stations and division chiefs.

Office of the Assistant to the Director. Under the reorganization of August 1, 1919, the Assistant to the Director is in direct charge of the Operations Branch, and responsible to the Director for all of the non-research or business work of the bureau.

Operations Branch. The Operations Branch, under the immediate supervision of the Assistant to the Director, includes the following divisions:
> Division of Office Administration
> Division of Education and Information
> Division of Mine-rescue Cars and Stations
> Government Fuel Yard

Division of Office Administration. At the head of the

Division of Office Administration is the Chief Clerk, who has charge of routine administrative matters at the central office and control of the methods of office administration at all stations and field offices as well as advisory responsibility as to bureau personnel, pay, and promotion of clerical and labor employees throughout the bureau. This division is composed of the following sections:

>   Personnel
>   Accounts
>   Legal
>   Mails and Files
>   Property and Shipments
>   Mimeograph

The Personnel Section (which is actually the Chief Clerk's office acting as a "section" only in name) handles all correspondence relating to appointments, leaves of absence, applications for transfer, and the maintenance of records relating thereto, as well as the compilation of miscellaneous tabular statements regarding personnel and such current reports as may be required from time to time.

The Section of Accounts is responsible for all matters relating to accounting and auditing work of the bureau. It keeps appropriation and allotment records, and prepares monthly statements for the information of the officers responsible for work under the various allotments. It examines all accounts presented for payment and passes on all vouchers payable.

The Legal Section prepares and examines contracts, leases, and agreements, correspondence relating to legal matters and United States mining laws, communications to the Attorney General and the Comptroller-General; follows legislation in Congress of interest to the bureau; assists in drafting proposed legislation in which the bureau is interested; and prepares legal opinions for guidance of administrative and accounting officers.

The duties of the Section of Mails and Files consist of

receiving, opening, and distributing all incoming mail to the various divisions and employees of the service, and handling of all outgoing mail, and the maintenance of correspondence and data files. The messenger force is under the direction of this section.

The Section of Property and Shipments keeps a record of location and condition of all non-expendable property of the bureau; ships and receives all express and freight of the Washington office; and directs the labor force in that office.

The Mimeograph Section is a service unit for the work done on the following machines: mimeograph, multigraph, mimescope, photostat, blueprint machine, addressograph, addressing machine, graphotype, paper cutting-machine, paper-trimming machine, stitching machine, and sealing machine.

Division of Education and Information. In 1919 the following sections of the bureau's work were assembled in a new Division of Education and Information, with a mining engineer in charge:

> Editorial
> Publications
> Library
> Reference Files
> Motion Pictures and Exhibits
> Statistical
> Codification of Mining Laws

This division was created because Section 2 of the organic act creating the bureau enjoins it "to disseminate information concerning these subjects [mining and preparation, treatment, and utilization of mineral substances] in such manner as will best carry out the purpose of this act."

The dissemination of scientific information is obviously a function quite distinct from that involved in the securing of such information through investigation and study and requires a different type of experience and ability. The work of the bureau in the production of new information through research and study had grown to such an extent that it called for a better organization and equipment for the dissemination of the results of its investigations. An additional reason for giving greater attention to this phase of the bureau's work is the fact that the increase in the cost of paper and of labor had led to a great increase in the expense of dissemination through printed publications.

The chief of this division is responsible for establishing and maintaining contact with other branches of the national government and with the public. He makes recommendations as to the nature and scope of publications and exhibits, and for putting the results of investigations into serviceable form for government departments, coöperating agencies, and the general public.

The Editorial Section, which is conducted by an engineer, is responsible for the editing of manuscripts and other official matter released for printing, and the determination of engraving processes and methods of illustration to be used in publications. The results of the bureau's investigations and researches appear not only in the official publications, but also in part in the technical press.

Brief reports on minor investigations or important phases of principal investigations are assembled and prepared for issuance under the direct supervision of the chief of the division, by an engineer on the staff of his personal office.

The Publications Section is concerned with the distribution of the publications showing the results of the bureau's activities and with the dissemination of information helpful to the mining interests and mine workers. These publications include Bulletins, Technical Papers, Miners' Circulars, and other printed or mimeographed articles and reports. A major function of the Publications Section is the answering of general letters of inquiry addressed to the bureau on all phases of the mineral industry. About one hundred thousand letters are received by this section annually; most of them are answered in the section and a few are referred to the technical divisions for a more detailed reply.

ORGANIZATION

The Section of Motion Pictures and Exhibits arranges for and manages exhibits made by the bureau at national and international expositions; secures coöperation of mineral industry companies and individuals, and arranges for and directs the production of educational motion pictures relating to the mineral industry, and also for the showing of the bureau's motion pictures before audiences connected with or interested in the mineral industry. The use of motion pictures is an important feature in the work of promoting health and safety among miners. Most of the films have been produced with little or no expense to the bureau.

The Section of Statistics compiles for issuance annually reports on accidents in coal mines, metal mines, quarries, and metallurgical plants. These reports contain data showing by states the number of workers in the industry, the number and causes of fatal accidents, and (except for coal mines) the number and causes of non-fatal injuries, as well as comparable accident rates and other accident data interpretations. The section also compiles for issuance annually figures showing the quantity of explosives of different kinds used in each state in coal and other mining work.

The work of the Section of Codification of Mining Laws is indicated by its title and has been previously described.

The Library collects, maintains, and makes available for the use of bureau employees and other persons, printed matter relating to subjects with which the bureau is concerned. Its service includes the Washington office and field stations and offices. There are branch libraries at the experiment stations. The various collections number about 17,500 volumes.

The Reference Files Section maintains a general reference and technical information file on matters pertaining to the mining and mineral industries.

Division of Mine-rescue Cars and Stations. The work of the mine-rescue cars and stations was transferred in 1919 from the Mining Division to a new Division of Mine-rescue Cars and Stations, under a mining engineer with headquarters at Pittsburgh (Pa.). This division is charged with the operation of all mine-rescue cars and stations, the rendering of assistance at mine explosions, fires, and other accidents, the testing and development of mine-rescue apparatus, the training of miners in first-aid and rescue methods, and the conduct of first-aid and rescue contests.

When not engaged in rescue and first-aid work, engineers of this division may be assigned to investigative work under the Mining Division. Similarly, engineers in the Mining Division may be assigned to rescue and first-aid work.

For purposes of safety work the country is divided into safety districts, each with a district engineer in charge. These districts and their headquarters are:

District	Headquarters
A. Northern Appalachian,	Pittsburgh, Pa.
B. Southern Appalachian,	Birmingham, Ala.
C. Eastern Interior,	Vincennes, Ind.
D. Lake Superior,	Minneapolis, Minn.
E. Southwestern,	McAlester, Okla.
F. Rocky Mountain,	Denver, Colo.
G. Northern Rocky Mountain (or Intermountain)	Salt Lake, Utah.
H. Northern Pacific,	Seattle, Wash.[2]
I. Southern Pacific,	Berkeley, Calif.

There are also ten mine-rescue stations distributed throughout the mining districts, as follows:

District	Station	Special Equipment	Established
A.	Pittsburgh, Pa.	Training gallery; motor rescue truck	(1908)
A.	Wilkes-Barre, Pa.		(1920)
A.	Norton, Va.	Motor rescue truck	(1910)
B.	Birmingham, Ala.		(1909 and 1918)
B.	Knoxville, Tenn.	Motor rescue truck	(1918)
C.	Vincennes, Ind.	Training gallery; motor truck	(1918)
C.	Evansville, Ind.	Training gallery	(1910)
E.	McAlester, Okla.	Training gallery; motor truck	(1909)
H.	Seattle, Wash.		
I.	Berkeley, Calif.	Motor rescue truck	(1919)

The bureau operates ten mine-rescue cars, which are distributed as follows:

[2] Temporary headquarters at Denver.

ORGANIZATION

District	Car. No.	Headquarters
A.	3	Pittsburgh, Pa.
A.	8	Huntington, W. Va.
C.	9	Terre Haute, Ind.
C.	7	Des Moines, Iowa.
D.	10	Ironwood, Mich.
E.	4	Pittsburgh, Kans.
F.	2	Raton, N. Mex.
G.	11	Rock Springs, Wyo.
H.	5	Butte, Mont.
I.	1	Reno, Nev.

Cars 1, 2, 5, 9, 10, and 11 are all-steel cars purchased since 1917. Cars 3, 4, 7, and 8 are old wooden Pullman cars secured in 1910. Car 6, an old wooden Pullman car, was worn out and retired from service in 1919.

Government Fuel Yard. The maintenance and operation of the Government Fuel Yard at Washington is entrusted to a chief engineer. This yard was begun in 1918 and the installation was completed in 1919. It supplies coal to all national and municipal plants, except the Navy Yard, within and near the District of Columbia,—the distribution points being over seven hundred in number.[3]

Investigations Branch. In the Investigations Branch are grouped the several technical divisions and also the division of mining experiment stations and field offices, all under the immediate jurisdiction of the Assistant Director. The divisions are as follows:

Mining
Mineral Technology
Metallurgy
Fuels
Petroleum and Natural Gas
Mining Experiment Stations

The chief of each technical division acts as a consulting engineer on the problems germane to his work arising in any division, and as such he is consulted directly by all other division chiefs, section chiefs, district engineers, and station

[3] This yard is particularly described in Annual Report, 1920, pp. 137-49.

superintendents. He advises with administrative officers as to the qualifications of personnel to whom such problems may be assigned and the methods of investigation to be employed, and he makes inspections of investigation work in progress. He also passes on all reports of investigations in his field submitted for publication. Each division chief is also subject to assignment by the Director to the administration as well as technical control of work of a special nature within the field of his special knowledge.

Chief Surgeon. The office of Chief Surgeon was created in February, 1920, with headquarters in Washington, attached to the Investigations Branch. The medical personnel, including the Chief Surgeon, is detailed from the United States Public Health Service under a coöperative agreement. This arrangement succeeded a slightly different form of coöperation between the two bureaus for the study of accidents and health hazards in mining.

The investigative work of the Chief Surgeon's office consists of a study of all the health hazards of the mining, quarrying, metallurgical, and allied industries. The problems for investigation are assigned by the Director according to their relative urgency or importance.

The investigations are carried on at the various experiment stations of the bureau and in the field. Practically all the investigations are made in coöperation with bureau engineers. From time to time consulting surgeons, physiologists, and other specialists are employed to study some of the problems or to assist or advise the regular personnel in making investigations.

Mining Division. The field of work of the Mining Division includes all investigations relating to the mining and preparation of coal at the mine; all investigations dealing with metal mining engineering problems in production and such associated matters as the Director may assign; the testing and use of explosives; safety in mines, quarries, mills, smelters, and other works, including the use of safety devices and appliances in and around mines. The administrative head is the Chief Mining Engineer, stationed at Washington, who has a mining engineer as an assistant. Coal-mining investigations are directed by a Coal-Mining Engineer and explosives investigations by an Explosives Engineer, both stationed at Pittsburgh and reporting to the Chief Mining Engineer. Consulting engineers and chemists, are employed from time to time. The division advisory committee is made up of the Chief Mechanical Engineer, the Chief Mineral Technologist, the Chief Metallurgist, the Supervisor of Stations, the Chief of the Division of Mine-Rescue Cars and Stations, and the Chief Explosives Chemist. The Federal Mine Inspector for Alaska and the mining supervisors on coal and certain other mines on the public domain serve under the Chief Mining Engineer.

While the division headquarters is Washington, much of the work is done at experiment stations, particularly Pittsburgh, and in the field. Field investigations are conducted by field engineers through the district engineers. For this purpose the country is divided into nine mining districts, which are identical with the mine-safety districts already described [4] and under the same district engineers. The district engineer in charge of the Rocky Mountain District is also Supervising Mining Engineer on technical investigations in the four western districts.

Division of Mineral Technology. A Chief Mineral Technologist is in charge of the Division of Mineral Technology. The work of this division includes problems of physics, chemistry, and engineering involved in the production and refining of metals other than ferrous, precious, and major non-ferrous metals, and in the production and preparation of non-metals other than petroleum, natural gas, and fuels.

Its work has to do, for example, with the problems in production and refining of radium, vanadium, and platinum, preparation of alloy steels, quarrying and preparation of build-

[4] See page 44.

ing stones, production and utilization of clays, graphite, and potash.

This work is done at ,Washington, at experiment stations, and in the field, through permanent employees and consulting engineers and chemists. A large number of special problems in the mining and metallurgical fields, the solution of which involves especially work in physics and chemistry are referred to the chief of this division. The advisory committee is composed of the Chief Mining Engineer, the Chief of the Division of Education and Information, and the Supervisor and Assistant Supervisor of Stations.

The field office at Ithaca, New York, is subordinate to this division.

Metallurgical Division. The Metallurgical Division was created in 1915. The Chief Metallurgist is stationed at Washington, but most of the work of the division is done at the several experiment stations scattered throughout the country. An Assistant Chief Metallurgist is stationed at San Francisco and charged with immediate technical control of metallurgical investigations at the Western experiment stations. Consulting engineers and chemists are engaged from time to time. In general, this division is concerned with the major metals and their economical reduction from low-grade and complex ores.

Fuels Division. A Chief Mechanical Engineer, with headquarters in Washington, is the head of the Fuels Division, which like the other technical divisions, conducts much of its work at experiment stations and in the field, both through regular personnel and through consulting engineers and chemists. This work has to do with: problems relating to fuel preparation, treatment, and utilization, including combustion; fuel inspection and coal analysis; preparation and use of powdered fuel; combustion of coal and other fuel to avoid smoke nuisances; manufacture of briquettes; coking and semicoking of coal; production and use of artificial gas and utilization of natural gas and petroleum for steam generation;

utilization of lignite and peat; and problems relating to mechanical and electrical equipment in mines, including the testing and approval of miners' lamps. A close relation is maintained with other government departments in giving advice as to proper selection, purchase, and methods of firing coal and other fuel.

The Chief Mining Engineer, Chief Petroleum Technologist, Supervisor of Stations, and the engineer in charge of the Government Fuel Yard comprise the advisory committee.

Division of Petroleum and Natural Gas. Provision for intensive work in petroleum technology was first made by Congress in 1914, and the creation of the Division of Petroleum and Natural Gas was the result. This division is under a Chief Petroleum Technologist, at Washington, who has the usual quota of consulting engineers and chemists. It is concerned with all problems relating to the drilling of wells, the production and transportation of petroleum and natural gas, and the refining of petroleum, as well as the chemistry and engineering technology of petroleum products.

The advisory committee includes the Chief Mechanical Engineer, Supervisor of Stations, Chief Mineral Technologist, and Chief of the Division of Education and Information.

The field offices subordinate to this division are at Dallas, (Tex.), Shreveport, (La.), Denver and Boulder (Colo.), Casper (Wyo.), Winnett (Mont.), San Francisco and Bakersfield (Calif.).

The Oil and Gas Supervisor and field force on the leasing work report to the Chief Petroleum Technologist.

Division of Mining Experiment Stations. The need for closer coördination between the technical divisions and the experiment stations led to the consolidation of those stations in a Division of Mining Experiment Stations in 1919. The head of this division is a Supervisor who, at present, is also Chief Metallurgist, and under him is an Assistant Chief Metallurgist. There are thirteen stations, each under a superintendent. They are as follows:

Location	Subjects Under Investigation
Bartlesville, Okla.	Petroleum
Berkeley, Calif.	Metallurgy
Birmingham, Ala. (Laboratory at Tuscaloosa, Ala.)	Non-metallic minerals and coke by-products
Columbus, Ohio	Ceramics
Fairbanks, Alaska	Alaska lode and placer mining and metallurgy
Minneapolis, Minn.	Iron mining and beneficiation
Pittsburgh, Pa.	Fuels, coal mining, explosives, general chemical and service laboratories
Reno, Nev.	Rare and precious metals
St. Louis, Mo. (Laboratory at Rolla, Mo.)	Lead and zinc mining and metallurgy
Salt Lake, Utah	Metal mining and metallurgy; smoke abatement
Seattle, Wash.	Electrometallurgy; ceramics, coal-washing, mining methods
Tucson, Ariz	Copper mining and metallurgy
Urbana, Ill.	Coal mining, fuels, coal preparation

The work of the Pittsburgh station may be grouped under general heads as follows: Testing of explosives, testing of explosibility of coal dusts, coal mining investigations, mine gases, electrical equipment, mine-safety and rescue work, metallurgy of non-ferrous metals, petroleum research laboratory, tests of fuels, mechanical equipment, and chemical research laboratory.

There is a field office at Moscow, Idaho, for coöperative studies with the University of Idaho on mining and metallurgical problems.

APPENDIX 1

OUTLINE OF ORGANIZATION

Explanatory Note

The Outlines of Organization have for their purpose to make known in detail the organization and personnel possessed by the several services of the national government to which they relate. They have been prepared in accordance with the plan followed by the President's Commission on Economy and Efficiency in the preparation of its outlines of the organization of the United States government.[1] They differ from those outlines, however, in that while the commission's report showed only organization units, the presentation herein has been carried far enough to show the personnel embraced in each organization unit.

These outlines are of value not merely as an effective means of making known the organization of the several services. If kept revised to date by the services they constitute exceedingly important tools of administration. They permit the directing personnel to see at a glance the organization and personnel at their disposition. They establish definitely the line of administrative authority and enable each employee to know his place in the system. They furnish the *essential basis* for making plans for determining costs by organization division and subdivision. They afford the data for a consideration of the problem of classifying and standardizing personnel and compensation. Collectively, they make it possible to determine the number and location of organization divisions of any particular kind, as for example—laboratories, libraries, blueprint rooms, or any other kind of plant possessed by the national government, to what services they are attached and

[1] House Doc. 458, 62d Cong., 2d Sess. 1912—2 vols.

where they are located, or to determine what services are maintaining stations at any city or point in the United States. The institute hopes that upon the completion of the proposed series it will be able to prepare a complete classified statement of the technical and other facilities at the disposal of the government. The present monographs will then furnish the details regarding the organization, equipment, and work of the institutions so listed and classified.

OUTLINE OF ORGANIZATION
BUREAU OF MINES
DEPARTMENT OF THE INTERIOR
AUGUST 15, 1921

Organization Units; *Classes of Employees;*	Number	*Annual Salary* *Rate* [2]
1. General Administration		
1. Office proper of the Director		
Director	1	$6,000
Private Secretary to the Director	1	2,160
Clerk	1	1,620
2. Special Technical Assistant to the Director		
Mining and Metallurgical Engineer	1	4,500
Clerk	1	1,440
3. Office of the Assistant Director		
Assistant Director	1	5,500
Clerk	1	1,500
Chief Explosives Chemist	1	4,800
Junior Clerk	1	1,320
Chief Surgeon (U. S. Public Health Service)	1	4,000
Clerk	1	1,500
4. Office of the Assistant to the Director		
Assistant to the Director	1	4,000
Mining Engineer	1	4,000
Mine Safety Commissioner	1	3,300
Clerk	2	1,620
Assistant Petroleum Engineer	1	3,600
Executive Secretary—Leasing Act Enforcement	1	2,100
Stenographer and Typist	1	1,200
Engineer Draftsman	1	1,920
2. Operations Branch		

[2] Net, or without the temporary "bonus" or additional compensation of 60 per cent on classes below $400, of $240 on classes of $400 to $2,500, and of an amount necessary to make the total compensation $2,740 on classes of $2,500 to $2,740. This is subject to minor exceptions in special cases.

OUTLINE OF ORGANIZATION 53

1. Division of Office Administration
    1. Office of the Chief Clerk

Chief Clerk	1	3,000
Junior Clerk	1	1,380

    2. Personnel Section

	1	1,200

    3. Section of Accounts

Accountant	1	2,400
Auditor	1	2,400
Senior Clerk	1	2,100
	1	1,920
	1	1,800
Clerk	1	1,680
	1	1,600
	1	1,560
Junior Clerk	1	1,400
	2	1,200
Under Clerk	1	1,200

    4. Legal Section

Law Examiner	1	1,980
Junior Clerk	1	1,320

    5. Section of Mails and Files

Clerk	1	1,920
	1	1,680
Junior Clerk	1	1,320
	1	1,200
Under Clerk	1	1,140
Laborer	1	840
Messenger	2	600
	2	510

    6. Section of Property and Shipments

Clerk	1	1,620
Junior Clerk	1	1,200
Unskilled Laborer	2	720

    7. Mimeograph Section

Clerk	1	1,440
Multigraph Operator	1	1,380
Junior Clerk	1	1,200
Addressograph Operator	1	1,080
	1	900
Mimeograph and Photograph Operator	1	1,080
Messenger	1	600
	1	510

    8. Helium Accounts Section

Clerk	1	2,000

2. Division of Education and Information
    1. Office of the Engineer in Charge

Mining Engineer	1	4,240
	1	2,220
Mining and Metallurgical Engineer	1	2,160
Junior Clerk	1	1,380

THE BUREAU OF MINES

- 2. Editorial Section
    - Engineer — 1 — 3,000
    - Illustrator — 1 — 1,860
    - Assistant Editor — 1 — 1,800
    - Editorial Assistant — 1 — 1,560
    - Junior Clerk — 1 — 1,380
- 3. Publications Section
    - Senior Clerk — 1 — 2,220
    - Junior Clerk — 1 — 1,380
    - — 1 — 1,320
    - Under Clerk — 1 — 1,140
    - — 3 — 1,100
- 4. Library
    - Assistant Librarian — 1 — 1,740
    - Junior Clerk — 1 — 1,320
- 5. Reference Files Section
    - Copyist Topographical Draftsman — 1 — 1,320
    - Junior Clerk — 1 — 1,260
- 6. Section of Motion Pictures and Exhibits
    - Safety Engineer — 1 — 3,240
- 7. Statistical Section
    - Mine-Accident Statistician — 1 — 2,400
    - Statistical Assistant — 2 — 1,500
    - Clerk — 1 — 1,500
    - Under Clerk — 1 — 1,140
    - — 1 — 1,000
    - Typist — 1 — 1,000
- 8. Mining Law Section
    - Law Examiner — 1 — 3,300
    - Junior Clerk — 1 — 1,320

3. Division of Mine Rescue Cars and Stations
   1. Office of Mine Safety Engineer, Pittsburgh, Pa.
      - Mine Safety Engineer — 1 — 4,240
      - Junior Clerk — 2 — 1,320
      - — 2 — 3,120
   2. Northern Appalachin Safety District
      1. Mine Safety Station, Pittsburgh, Pa.
         - Foreman Miner — 1 — 1,800
         - Foreman Miner, Detached — 1 — 1,800
         - Engrosser — 1 — 1,200
         - Mechanic Helper — 1 — 960
      2. Mine Safety Station, Wilkes-Barre, Pa.
         - Foreman Miner — 1 — 1,800
      3. Mine Safety Car No. 3, Pittsburgh, Pa.
         - Foreman Miner — 1 — 1,740
         - First Aid Miner — 1 — 1,440
         - Clerk — 1 — 1,260
         - Cook — 1 — 780

OUTLINE OF ORGANIZATION

    4. Mine Safety Station, Norton, Va.
        Foreman Miner   1   1,800
        First Aid Miner   1   1,440
    5. Mine Safety Car No. 8, Huntington, W. Va.
        Foreman Miner   1   1,800
        First Aid Miner   1   1,440
        Cook   1   780
3. Southern Appalachin Safety District
    1. Mine Safety Station, Birmingham, Ala.
        Mining Engineer   1   3,240
        Foreman Miner   1   1,740
        Under Clerk   1   900
        Laborer   1 (per diem)   a 2
    2. Mine Safety Station, Knoxville, Tenn.
        Foreman Miner   1   1,700
4. Eastern Interior Safety District
    1. Mine Safety Station, Vincennes, Ind.
        District Engineer   1   4,000
        Foreman Miner   1   1,800
        First Aid Miner   1   1,500
    2. Mine Safety Station, Evansville, Ind.
        Foreman Miner   1   1,800
    3. Mine Safety Car No. 6, Terre Haute, Ind.
        Car Engineer   1   3,000
        Surgeon   1   3,120
        Foreman   1   1,740
        First Aid Miner   1   1,440
        Junior Clerk   1   1,260
        Cook   1   780
    4. Mine Safety Car No. 7, Des Moines, Iowa
        Foreman Miner   1   1,800
        First Aid Miner   1   1,500
        Cook   1   780
5. Lake Superior Safety District
    1. Mine Safety Car No. 10, Ironwood, Mich.
        Car Engineer   1   3,000
        Surgeon   1   3,120
        Foreman Miner   1   1,740
        First Aid Miner   1   1,440
        Junior Clerk   1   1,200
        Cook   1   780
6. Southwestern Safety District
    1. Mine Safety Station, McAlester, Okla.
        Foreman Miner   1   1,800

Laborer	1 (per diem)	a 2

 2. Mine Safety Car. No. 4, Pittsburgh, Kans.

Foreman Miner	1	1,800
First Aid Miner	1	1,440
Cook	1	780

7. Rocky Mountain Safety District
 1 Mine Safety Car, No. 2, Raton, N. Mex.

Car Engineer	1	2,500
Foreman Miner	1	1,740
First Aid Miner	1	1,440
Junior Clerk	1	1,200
Cook	1	780

 2. Mine Safety Car No. 5, Butte, Mont.

Car Engineer	1	3,000
Foreman Miner	1	1,740
First Aid Miner	1	1,440
Junior Clerk	1	1,260
Cook	1	780

8. Intermountain (or Northern Rocky Mountain Safety District
 1. Mine Safety Car No. 11, Rock Springs, Wyo.

Car Engineer	1	3,000
Surgeon	1	3,120
Acting Foreman Miner	1	1,500
First Aid Miner	1	1,500
Junior Clerk	1	1,200
Cook	1	780

9. Northern Pacific Safety District
 1. Mine Safety Station, Seattle, Wash.

Foreman Miner	1	1,800

10. Southern Pacific Safety District
 1. Mine Safety Station, Berkeley, Calif.

Miner	1	1,800
First Aid Miner	1	1,440
Junior Clerk	1	1,380
Mechanic	1 (per hour)	a 35c

 2. Mine Safety Car No. 1, Reno, Nev.

Car Engineer	1	3,000
Foreman Miner	1	1,800
First Aid Miner	1	1,440
Junior Clerk	1	1,260
Cook	1	780

4. Government Fuel Yard
 1. Office of Chief Engineer

---

[a] When actually employed. Maximum $300 per annum.

OUTLINE OF ORGANIZATION

Chief Engineer	1	4,240
Assistant to Chief Engineer	1	2,100
Fuel Inspector	1	2,040
Superintendent of Fuel Distribution	1	1,800
Senior Clerk	1	1,860
Junior Clerk	1	1,400
	1	1,380
	1	1,260
	5	1,200
Under Clerk (temp.)	1	1,080
	1	1,020
Bookkeeping Machine Operator (temp.)	1	1,080
Calculating Machine Operator	1	1,080
Classified Laborer	1	1,200
Accountant	1	(per hour) [a] 1.50

2. Yards

Senior Clerk	1	2,040
Fuel Inspector	1	1,740
Stacker and Conveyor Operator	1	1,560
Fireman-Watchman	2	720
Watchman	2	(per diem) [a] 4
Coal Conveyor Expert	1	(per hour) [a] 10
Laborer Max. 30 aver.	14	(per hour) [a] 40c

3. Garage

Superintendent	1	1,800
Foreman Auto Mechanic	1	1,680
Auto Mechanic	2	1,500
	1	1,440
	2	1,380
	2	1,260
Blacksmith	1	1,380
Machanic's Helper	1	1,020
Junior Clerk	1	1,320
Skilled Laborer	1	1,020
Watchman	1	840
	2	(per diem) [a] 4
Fireman	1	1,200
Chauffeurs Max.35; aver.	16	(per hour) [b] 41-44c
Laborer Max.6; aver.	5	(per hour) [b] 40c

5. Enforcement of Operating Regulations under General Leasing Act
  1. Bakersville, Calif.

Deputy Supervisor of Oil and Gas Operations	1	4,140
Engineer Draftsman	1	2,100
Gauger	1	2,100
Junior Oil Clerk	1	1,500

[a] When actually employed. Maximum $300 per annum.
[b] When actually employed.

2. Caspar, Wyo.
   Deputy Supervisor of Oil and Gas
      Operations ... 1 ... 4,140
   Expert Driller ... 1 ... 3,600
   Chief Gauger ... 1 ... 3,600
   Gauger ... 3 ... 2,100
   Assistant Petroleum Engineer ... 1 ... 2,100
   Junior Clerk ... 1 ... 1,500
3. Denver, Colo.
   1. Mining Operations
      Deputy Supervisor ... 1 ... 4,000
      Technical Examiner ... 1 ... 3,600
      Junior Clerk ... 1 ... 1,200
   2. Oil and Gas Operations
      Supervisor ... 1 ... 4,800
      Associate Natural Gas Engineer ... 1 ... 3,600
      Engineer Draftsman ... 1 ... 2,100
      Senior Oil Clerk ... 1 ... 1,680
      Junior Oil Clerk ... 1 ... 1,260
   4. Shreveport, La.
      Deputy Supervisor (Vacancy)
      Petroleum Engineer ... 1 ... 3,300
      Junior Oil Clerk ... 1 ... 1,500
   5. Winett, Mont.
      Oil Recovery Engineer ... 1 ... 3,600
      Gauger ... 1 ... 2,100
3. Investigations Branch
   1. Mining Division
      1. Office of Chief Mining Engineer
         Chief Mining Engineer ... 1 ... 5,400
         Mining Engineer ... 1 ... 3,840
         Metal Mining Engineer ... 1 ... 4,000
         Clerk ... 1 ... 1,560
         Junior Clerk ... 1 ... 1,440
            ... 1 ... 1,320
      2. District Engineers
         Supervising Mining Engineer, F, Denver Colo. ... 1 ... 4,240
         Junior Clerk, F, Denver Colo. ... 1 ... 1,200
         Metal Mining Engineer, G, Salt Lake, Utah ... 1 ... 3,600
         Stenographer ... 1 ... 900
         H, Seattle, Wash. (Vacancy)
         Mining Engineer, I, Berkeley, Calif. ... 1 ... 4,000
      3. Inspection of Mines in Alaska
         Federal Mine Inspector for Alaska ... 1 ... 3,000
         Clerk ... 1 ... 1,500
   2. Division of Mineral Technology
      1. Office of Chief Mineral Technologist

OUTLINE OF ORGANIZATION

Chief Mineral Technologist; Chief Chemist	1		5,000
Assistant Chief Chemist	1		3,650
Mineral Technologist	1		3,600
Chemist	1		3,000
Junior Clerk	1		1,440
	2		1,200

2 Cyrogenic Laboratory
  1. Mechanical Section

Mechanical Engineer	1		4,000
Machinist	2		2,100
	1		1,600
Junior Clerk	1		1,380
Laborer (temp.)	1	(per hour)	40c

  2. Chemical Section

Physical Chemist	1		3,840
	1		3,340
Laboratory Aid	1		960

  3. Helium Repurification Plant, Langley Field, Va.

Mechanical Engineer	1	(per mo.)	350
Assistant Mechanical Engineer (temp.)	1	(per mo.)	210
Assistant Engineer (temp.)	1	(per mo.)	150
Carpenter (temp.)	1	(per mo.)	135
Gas Operator (temp.)	1	(per mo.)	125
Steam Fitter's Helper	1	(per mo.)	80
Rigger	1	(per mo.)	80
Stenographer (temp.)	1	(per diem) [a]	5
Draftsman	1	(per hour) [a]	1

  4. Helium Laboratory, Fort Worth, Tex.

Chemist	1		2,700
Assistant Chemist	1		2,280

  5. Field Office, Ithaca, N. Y.

Chief Alloy Chemist	1		4,240
Assistant Alloy Chemist	1		2,500
Junior Clerk	1	(per diem) [a]	4

3. Metallurgical Division
  1. Office of Chief Metallurgist (and Supervisor of Stations)

4. Fuels Division
  1. Office of Chief Mechanical Engineer

Chief Mechanical Engineer	1		5,400
Mechanical Engineer	1		3,120
Mechanical Draftsman	1		2,100
Junior Clerk	1		1,320

  2. Fuel Inspection

Assistant Fuel Engineer	1		2,500

[a] When actually employed.

Junior Clerk	1	1,380
	1	1,260
Coal Yard Foreman	1	1,260
Coal Inspector and Sampler	1	1,200

3. Lignite Investigation, Hefron, N. Dak.

Fuel Engineer	1	3,800
Junior Fuel Chemist	1	1,560
Junior Aid in Chemistry	1	1,200

5. Division of Petroleum and Natural Gas
   1. Office of the Chief Petroleum Technologist

Chief Petroleum Technologist	1	5,000
Petroleum Technologist	1	3,840
	2	3,000
Petroleum Economist	1	2,400
Junior Clerk	1	1,380
	1	1,260
	2	1,200

   2. Petroleum Laboratory

Petroleum Chemist	1	3,300
Physical Laboratory Helper	1	1,380
Junior Chemist	1	[a] 1,800

   3. Field Office, Dallas, Tex.

Petroleum Engineer	1	4,140
Oil Recovery Engineer	1	3,600
Expert Driller	1	3,600
Assistant Petroleum Technologist	1	2,820
Receipt Clerk	1	1,560

   4. Field Office, San Francisco, Calif.

Petroleum Engineer	1	4,020
Oil Recovery Engineer	1	3,600
Illustrative Draftsman	1	1,980
Junior Analytical Chemist	1	1,740
Chemical Laboratorian	1	1,560
Clerk	1	1,620
Editorial Assistant	1	1,320
Junior Clerk	1	1,200

   5. Field Staff: Coöperative Work, Boulder, Colo.
      Oil Shale Technologist

6. Division of Mining Experiment Stations
   1. Office of Supervisor of Stations

Supervisor of Stations (and Chief Metallurgist)	1	5,000
Senior Clerk	1	1,860
Junior Clerk	1	1,380

[a] Salary paid by U. S. Shipping Board

OUTLINE OF ORGANIZATION

2. Mining Experiment Station, Pittsburgh, Pa.
    1. Administrative Section
        Superintendent; Supervising
            Chemist 1 5,000
        Senior Clerk 1 1,980
        Principal Clerk 1 1,860
        Research Reference Clerk ... 1 1,800
        Clerk 1 1,620
                                     1 1,560
        Junior Clerk 1 1,440
        Library Assistant 1 1,320
        Junior Clerk 2 1,320
                                     4 1,200
        Junior Computer 1 1,080
        Under Clerk 1 1,080
                                     2 1,020
        Stenographer and Typist 1 1,020
        Captain of the Watch 1 1,020
        Chauffeur 1 1,020
        Unskilled Laborer 1 1,020
        Under Clerk 1 960
                                     1 840
        Telephone Operator 1 900
        Unskilled Laborer 1 900
        Janitor 1 900
                                     1 840
        Watchman 3 780
        Messenger 2 600
                                     4 480
        Laborer 8 540
    2. Chemical Section
        1. Supervising Chemist's Office
            Associate Supervising Chemist (Vacancy)
            Glass Blower and Instrument Maker 1 1,920
            Laboratory Assistant ... 1 1,680
            Laboratory Helper 1 1,200
            Junior Clerk 1 1,320
                                     1 1,200
            Under Clerk 1 1,020
        2. General Analytical Laboratory
            Assistant Analytical Chemist 1 2,880
            Junior Analytical Chemist 1 2,220
            Junior Organic Chemist . 2 1,680
            Junior Clerk 1 1,440
        3. Coal Analyses Laboratory
            Chemist 1 3,240

Assistant Physical Chemist	1	3,240
Junior Analytical Chemist	1	1,560
Junior Chemist	1	1,500
Analyst	1	1,500
Laboratory Assistant	1	1,200
Laboratory Helper	1	1,200
Laboratory Aid	1	900
Clerk-Computer	1	1,440
	1	1,200
Typist	1	1,020

4. Coal and Coal Products

Chemist	1	3,480
Associate Chemist	1	3,360
Junior Analytical Chemist	1	1,680

5. Explosives Laboratory

Associate Explosives Chemist	1	3,360
Assistant Explosives Chemist	1	2,160
	1	1,920
Junior Analytical Chemist	1	1,800

6. Gas Laboratory

Assistant Gas Chemist	1	2,500
Junior Analytical Chemist	1	1,680
Junior Physical Chemist	1	1,560
Chemical Laboratorian	1	1,200
Laboratory Assistant	1	1,200

7. Gas Masks, Respirators, and Breathing Apparatus

Assistant Physical Chemist	1	2,500
Junior Analytical Chemist	1	1,800
Junior Physical Chemist	1	1,680

8. Microscopical Laboratory

Chemist	1	3,240
Petrographer	1	2,400

9. Physical Laboratory

Associate Physicist	1	3,480

10. Sulphur in Fuels

Asssociate Physical Organic Chemist	1	3,120
Junior Organic Chemist	1	1,560

3. Coal Mining Section

1. The Section Proper

Coal Mining Engineer	1	4,240
	1	3,120
Assistant Coal Mining		

OUTLINE OF ORGANIZATION 63

Engineer	1	2,120
Assistant Physicist	1	2,340
Assistant Fuel Chemist	1	1,900
Junior Clerk	1	1,200
Under Clerk	1	1,140
Chemical Laboratorian	1	1,080

2. Experimental Mine, Bruceton, Pa.

Coal Mine Superintendent	1		2,880
Carpenter	1	(per diem)	7.50
Mine Driver	1	(per diem)	7.12
Laborer ave.	18	(per diem) min. 5.93 max. 7.50	

4. Explosives Section
   1. Office of the Explosives Engineer

Explosives Engineer	1	3,600
Explosives Testing Engineer	1	3,240
Assistant Explosives Engineer	1	2,500
Computer	1	1,200
Junior Clerk	1	1,200

   2. Explosives Experiment Station

Assistant Mechanical Engineer	1	2,500
Assistant Explosives Engineer	1	2,100
	1	1,980
Junior Explosives Engineer	1	1,680
Carpenter	1	1,380
Shot Firer	1	1,080
Laborer	1 (per diem) [a]	4.72

5. Fuels Section

Fuel Engineer	1	4,200
	1	2,500
Assistant Fuel Engineer	1	2,280
	1	1,920
	1	1,800
Junior Fuel Engineer	1	1,680
Assistant Engineer	1	2,100
Assistant Chemical Engineer	1	1,800
	1	1,680
Junior Physicist	2	1,800
Ventilating Draftsman	1	1,800
Assistant Mechanical Engineer	1	1,740

[a] When actually employed.

Clerk	1	1,500
Computer	1	1,500
Observer and Computer in Fuel Analysis	1	1,320
Laboratory Helper	1	1,200
Mechanic	1	1,200
Fireman	1	1,080
Unskilled Laborer	1	1,020

6. Technical Service

Assistant Engineer	1	2,100
Draftsman	1	1,980
Photographer	1	1,680
Junior Photographer	1	1,140
Clerk	1	1,560
	1	1,080
Copyist Draftsman	1	1,260
	1	1,140
Apprentice Motion Picture Operator	1	840
Photostat Operator	1	660

7. Petroleum Section

Petroleum Chemist	1	4,000
Chemical Engineer	1	2,880
Organic Chemist	1	2,500
Assistant Refinery Engineer	1	2,500
Assistant Oil Shale Engineer	1	2,100
Laboratory Assistant	1	1,800
Junior Clerk	1	1,320

8. Electrical Section

Electrical Engineer	1	3,500
Assistant Electrical Engineer	1	1,980
Junior Electrical Engineer	1	1,800
	1	1,620
	1	1,500
Electrical Engineering Aid	1	1,440

9. Mechanical Section

Mechanical Mine Safety Engineer	1	2,500

10. Non-Ferrous Metals Section

Metallurgist	1	3,060
Assistant Chemist	1	1,920

11. Tunnel Gas Investigation

Mechanical Engineer	1	3,900

12. Shops, Power Plant, and Labor Service Section

1. Superintendent's Office

Superintendent	1	2,400

OUTLINE OF ORGANIZATION 65

2. Instrument Shop
    Foreman Instrument
      Maker   1   1,830
    Instrument Maker   1   1,710
                                  1   1,590
    Junior Instrument
      Maker   1   1,490
    Mechanician   1   1,530
                                  1   1,430
3. Carpenter Shop
    Millwright   1   1,500
    Carpenter   1   1,380
                                  1   1,320
4. Machine Shop
    Machinist   1   1,500
                                  1   1,080
    Machinist's Helper   1   900
    Plumber   1   1,440
    Electrician's Helper   1   1,320
5. Power Plant
    Fireman   4   1,020
    Oiler and Engine
      Runner   1   960
                                  1   840
6. Labor Force
    Labor Foreman   1   1,380
    Unskilled Laborer   1   960
                                  4   900
    Laborer   1   900
7. Garage
    Garage Foreman   1   1,380
    Garageman   1   900
    Apprentice Auto
      Mechanic   1   480

3. Mining Experiment Station,
   Bartlesville, Okla.
    Superintendent; Refinery
      Engineer   1   4,020
    Petroleum Technologist   1   4,000
    Petroleum Engineer   1   3,120
    Principal Clerk   1   1,800
    Junior Clerk   1   1,200
                                  1   960
    Engineer-Janitor   1   1,080
    Assistant Organic Chemist   1   ....[a]
    Junior Chemist   1   ....[a]
    Refinery Engineer   1   ....[a]
    Refinery Operator   1   ....[a]

4. Mining Experiment Station,

[a] On leave without pay on coöperative agreements.

Berkeley, Calif.
 Superintendent; Assistant
  Chief Metallurgist   1   4,800
 Physical Chemist   1   2,400
 Junior Clerk   1   1,200
  (temp.)   1   (per hour)[a]   60c
 Laboratory Helper   1   (per hour)   75c

5. Mining Experiment Station, Birmingham-Tuscaloosa, Ala.
 Superintendent (and District
  Engineer)   1   4,400
 Mineral Technologist   1   4,000
 Associate Physical Chemist   1   3,600
 Associate Metallurgical
  Chemist   1   2,160
 Junior Analytical Chemist
  (temp.)   1   (per mo.)   150
 Junior Clerk   1   1,500

6. Mining Experiment Station, Columbus, Ohio.
 Superintendent; Chief
  Ceramist   1   4,800
 Associate Chemist   1   4,000
 Ceramic Chemist   1   3,000
 Junior Ceramic Chemist   1   (per hour)[a]   .70
 Ceramic Assistant   1   1,740
     1   1,620
 Junior Ceramic Engineer
  (temp.)   1   1,560
 Laboratory Assistant   1   1,260
 Laboratory Aid (temp.)   1   (per mo.)   80
 Unskilled Laborer   1   900
 Senior Clerk   1   1,800
 Junior Clerk   1   1,320

7. Mining Experiment, Station, Fairbanks, Alaska.
 Superintendent; Mining
  Engineer   1   4,600
 Analytical Chemist and
  Mineralogist   1   3,240
 Assistant Mechanical Engineer   1   3,000
 Mechanic   1   1,920
 Senior Clerk   1   1,800
 Unskilled Laborer (temp.)   1   (per hour)[a]   .80
 Laborer   1   (per hour)[a]   .80

8. Mining Experiment Station, Minneapolis, Minn.
 Superintendent; Mineral
  Technologist   1   4,240
 Metallurgist   1   3,240

[a] When actually employed.

OUTLINE OF ORGANIZATION

Assistant Metallurgist	1		2,460
	1		1,980
Junior Analytical Chemist	1		1,500
Laboratory Aid (temp.)	1	(per mo.)	80
Senior Clerk	1		1,860
Unskilled Laborer	1		900

9. Mining Experiment Station, Reno, Nev.

Superintendent; Physical Chemist	1	4,240
Metallurgist	1	3,720
	1	1,800
Assistant Chemist	1	2,200
Assistant Physical Chemist	1	2,000
Principal Clerk	1	1,860
Janitor	1	840

10. Mining Experiment Station, St. Louis-Rolla, Mo.

Superintendent (acting); Mining Engineer (and District Engineer)	1		3,600
Metallurgist	1		3,780
Assistant Metallurgist	1		3,000
	1		2,280
Technical Examiner	1		3,600
Senior Clerk	1		1,860
Junior Clerk	1		1,200
Drill Runner (temp.)	2	(per mo.)	150

11. Mining Experiment Station, Salt Lake, Utah.

1. The Station Proper

Superintendent; Metallurgist	1	4,500
Hydro-Metallurgist	1	3,000
Ore Dressing Engineer	1	2,400
Assistant Chemist Metallurgical Assistant	1	2,040
Assistant Oil Shale Technologist	1	1,980
Clerk	1	1,740
Junior Clerk	1	1,200
Unskilled Laborer	1	960

2. Field Office, Moscow, Id.

Ore Dressing Engineer	1	2,400
Assistant Metallurgist (temp.)	1	1,800

12. Mining Experiment Station, Seattle, Wash.

Superintendent	1		[a] 3,840
Ceramist (temp.)	1	(per mo.)	300
Metallurgical Chemist	1		2,400

[a] When actually employed.

68 THE BUREAU OF MINES

Electro-Metallurgist	1	2,400
Mining Engineer	1	2,280
Junior Mining Engineer	1	1,680
Mechanician	1	1,500
Mill Mechanic	1	1,320
Clerk	1	1,500
Junior Clerk	1	[a] 1,260
Analyist (temp.)	1 (per mo.)	100

13. Mining Experiment Station, Tucson, Ariz.

Superintendent; Mining Engineer and Metallurgist	1	4,240
Metallurgist	1	3,840
Junior Chemist	1	1,800
Analyst	1	1,800
Senior Clerk	1	1,800
General Mechanic	1	1,200
Laboratory Aid	1	900

14. Mining Experiment Station, Urbana, Ill.

Superintendent	1	4,000
Illuminating Gas Engineer	1	3,240
Assistant Chemist	1	2,100
Assistant Mining Engineer	1	2,040
Under Clerk	1	1,020

7. U. S. Helium Plant No. 3, Petrolia, Tex.

   1. Office proper of Liquefaction Engineer

Liquefaction Engineer	1	7,500
Superintendent	1	4,000
Assistant Office Manager	1	2,160
Stenographer	1	1,800
Watchman	2 (per hour) [a]	.55c

   2. Laboratory

Chemist	1	1,800

   3. Plant

Assistant Liquefaction Engineer	1	3,900
Chief Engineer	1	3,600
Test Engineer	1	2,700
Senior Engineer	1	2,500
Mechanic	1	2,400

4. Consultants — *Per Diem* [a]

Ceramist	1	10
Chemist	1	10
	1 (per annum)	1
Metallurgical Chemist	1	8
Physical Chemist	1	10
	1	8
Junior Fuel Chemist	1 (per hour)	75c

[a] When actually employed.

OUTLINE OF ORGANIZATION

	1		2,500
Assistant Research Chemist	1		5
Economist	1		10
Mine Economist	1		10
Engineer	27		10
	1		8
Assistant Engineer	1		10
Chemical Engineer	2		10
	1	(per annum)	1
Coal Mining Engineer	1		10
Construction Engineer	1		10
Electrical Engineer	1		10
Explosives Engineer	1		10
Fuel Engineer	2		10
Mechanical Engineer	4		10
Metallurgical Engineer	1		10
Mining Engineer	15		10
	1	(per annum)	1
Petroleum Engineer	3		10
	1		8
Refinery Engineer	1		10
Metallurgist	10		10
Microscopist	1	(per hour)	1
Mining Expert	1		10
Petroleum Technologist	3		10
Physicist	1		10
Physiologist	3		10
Quarry Technologist	2		10
Statistician	1	(per hour)	1
Surgeon	5		10
Technologist	1		10

APPENDIX 2

CLASSIFICATION OF ACTIVITIES

Explanatory Note

The Classifications of Activities have for their purpose to list and classify in all practicable detail the specific activities engaged in by the several services of the national government. Such statements are of value from a number of standpoints. They furnish, in the first place, the most effective showing that can be made in brief compass of the character of work performed by the service to which they relate. Secondly, they lay a basis for a system of accounting and reporting that will permit of the showing of total expenditures classified according to activities. Finally, taken collectively, they make possible the preparation of a general or consolidated statement of the activities of the government as a whole. Such a statement will reveal in detail, not only what the government is doing, but the services in which the work is being performed. For example, one class of activities that would probably appear in such a classification is that of "scientific research." A subhead under this class would be "chemical research." Under this head would appear the specific lines of investigation under way and the services in which they were being prosecuted. It is hardly necessary to point out the value of such information in planning for future work and in considering the problem of the better distribution and coördination of the work of the government. The Institute has it in contemplation to attempt such a general listing and classification of the activities of the government upon the completion of the present series.

Classification of Activities

1. Promotion of Safety and Health in the Mining and Metallurgical Industries
    1. Investigation of accidents
    2. Research in accident-prevention
    3. Investigation of mine hazards
    4. Investigation of hygienic conditions
    5. Research for improvement of conditions affecting health, comfort, or efficiency of workers
    6. Operation of mine-safety stations and cars
    7. Training and information to the miner
2. Technological Researches and Investigations
    1. Mining
    2. Mineral technology
    3. Metallurgy
    4. Solid mineral fuels
    5. Petroleum and natural gas
3. Administration
    1. Inspection of mines and mine leases
    2. War minerals relief
    3. Government fuel yards
4. Compilation of Legal and Special Statistical Data needed in connection with the investigations of the bureau and for the industry.

APPENDIX 3

PUBLICATIONS

The Bureau of Mines publishes bulletins, technical papers, miners' circulars, a monthly statement of fatalities in coal mines, annual statements of metal-mine, quarry, coke-oven, and metallurgical plant accidents, the annual report of the Director, and miscellaneous publications, such as hand-books on special subjects, posters, charts, lists, and schedules.

The bulletins include those reports which present in detail the results of technical and scientific investigations. They are of interest primarily to engineers, chemists, mine officers, and other persons familiar with the subject discussed.

The technical papers are shorter and less formal than the bulletins. They give preliminary notice of the results of detailed investigations, or describe small incidental investigations.

Miners' circulars deal with such practical matters as accident prevention, rescue and first-aid methods, the safeguarding of health, and other topics that directly concern the workers in mines, mills, and metallurgical plants. They are written in simple non-technical English, and they are issued in large editions. A circular on first-aid for miners was printed in Italian, Polish, and Slovak, with the English version on opposite pages.

The annual report of the Director is a formal statement addressed to the Secretary of the Interior, showing the organization of the bureau, its activities, and the nature and results of its work, together with proposals for future undertakings. Of the first ten reports only three are indexed.

Up to the end of the fiscal year 1920 the bureau had issued

PUBLICATIONS

117 bulletins, 243 technical papers, and twenty-one miners' circulars.

Arrangements have been perfected with foreign and domestic government mining departments or bureaus, mining and technical libraries, and periodicals for an exchange of publications.

Monthly post cards are sent out notifying interested persons of the issuance of new publications, and from time to time descriptive circulars of the bureau's publications available for distribution are issued.

A ten-year record of publications distributed directly by the bureau is given below (copies sold by the Superintendent of Documents not included) :

Fiscal Year	Annual Reports	Bulletins	Technical Papers	Miners' Circulars	Miscellaneous	Total
1911	....	36,020	5,155	69,329	....	110,504
1912	2,022	96,762	56,903	351,849	....	507,536
1913	11,542	142,322	243,756	416,849	21,087	835,556
1914	8,319	154,706	226,320	559,322	90,926	1,039,603
1915	11,140	90,793	171,797	579,423	100,332	953,485
1916	9,892	97,095	174,631	318,002	93,636	693,256
1917	2,294	72,883	129,000	479,149	119,600	802,926
1918	1,894	81,374	168,411	91,459	185,294	528,432
1919	2,502	92,485	170,036	235,289	90,642	590,954
1920	1,375	67,793	183,847	453,154	106,692	813,061

Authority for the issuance of publications is given in Section 2 of the organic act of February 25, 1913: "That it shall be the province and duty of the Bureau of Mines, subject to the approval of the Secretary of the Interior, to . . . disseminate information concerning these subjects in such manner as will best carry out the purpose of this Act"; also in Section 3, which provides; "That the director of said bureau shall prepare and publish, subject to the direction of the Secretary of the Interior, under the appropriations made from time to time by congress, reports of inquiries and investigations, with appropriate recommendations of the bureau, concerning the nature, causes and prevention of accidents, and the improvement of conditions, methods and equipment with special reference to health, safety, and prevention of waste in the mining, quarrying, metallurgical and other mineral industries; the use of explosives and electricity, safety methods and appliances, and rescue and first-aid work in said industries; the causes and prevention of mine fires; and other subjects included under the provisions of this act." Further authority is granted in the joint resolution of June 25, 1910 (36 Stat. L., 883), which provides that the publications of the bureau shall be published in such editions as may be recommended by the Secretary, not to exceed ten thousand copies in the case of a first edition; also that whenever the edition of any of the publications shall have become exhausted and the demand for it continues, "there shall be published, on the requisition of the Secretary of the Interior, as many additional copies as the Secretary of the Interior may deem necessary to meet the demand."

A change of policy was instituted in 1919, the cause and nature of which are set forth in the annual report for 1920:

> The demands of the mining and allied industries upon the bureau for publications have been so great that it has been impossible under the appropriations granted by congress to keep on hand a supply of all of them for free distribution. The bureau, therefore, to meet the demands in some manner, has been compelled to affix a price on a few of its publications, and in such instances refers the applicants to the Superintendent of Documents, Government Printing Office, Washington, D. C., who is permitted by law to set a nominal price upon publications covering the cost of printing but not the cost of the investigations, which is borne by the Bureau of Mines. The bureau reasons that having made the investigations and obtained the valuable and timely data for the industries, and not then having money for the printing of the paper, it is to the best interests of the industries to request the Superintendent of Documents to print an edition for sale. . . .
>
> If the demands of the mining and allied industries continue to grow as in the past, and there is every evidence that they will, there will be increasing necessity, in order to give prompt

and efficient service, to have more and more of its publications printed under similar arrangements, a price being affixed and the papers sold through the Superintendent of Documents. The bureau has found that such a plan is acceptable to the industries in that the prompt and efficient service is not to be weighed against the nominal cost.

In addition to this sale of certain of its publications, the bureau, as a rule, intends to print only a first edition of its free reports, and after this is exhausted the applicants will be referred to the Superintendent of Documents, who is supposed to have an edition of each publication for sale. In this way the Superintendent of Documents is selling each year about 35,000 copies of Bureau of Mines publications.

The number of Bureau of Mines publications sold by the Superintendent of Documents up to July 1, 1920 was 344,395; and the receipts from these sales amounted to $36,129.

APPENDIX 4

PLANT AND EQUIPMENT

The central offices and three of the laboratories of the Bureau of Mines are located in the Interior Department Building, 18th, 19th, E, and F streets, N. W., Washington.

The laboratories in Washington are as follows:

The cyrogenic laboratory is maintained for the purpose of investigating fundamental physical and chemical problems involved in the production of helium on a commercial scale to meet the requirements of the Army and Navy. It is equipped with apparatus of semi-commercial size. It is proposed to make the facilities of this laboratory available to university investigators who wish to work on these or similar problems.

The petroleum laboratory is used for routine analyses of crude oil, fuel oil, kerosene, and gasoline for other government departments, and for conducting semi-annual surveys of motor gasoline sold throughout the United States.

The small mineral technology laboratory is used for two purposes. (1) The preliminary examination of mineral substances submitted to the bureau by other government agencies; (2) The carrying on of minor research problems in the utilization of the minerals, under the direct supervision of the Chief and Assistant Chief Mineral Technologist.

The Government Fuel Yard is located on rented land at Half and I streets, S. E., Washington, D. C. It has two railroad spurs, each with a capacity of sixteen cars, on a 1½ per cent grade. It is fully equipped for the economical handling of coal from the car to the consumer's bin, having track hoppers, belt conveyors, an automatic electric conveyor scale, self-clearing bins, traveling hopper, locomotive crane, reserve storage space, and a fleet of motor trucks. This equip-

PLANT AND EQUIPMENT

ment has an unloading capacity from cars of 300 tons an hour, from bins into trucks of 1200 to 2000 tons daily, and a storage capacity of 20,000 tons. The cost of the yard and its fixed equipment was $260,000. For the storage and repair of the motor equipment, a rented garage with a machine shop attached is maintained at 58 B street, S. W. The cost of automobile trucks and garage equipment was $170,000.

Bakersfield, California, is the headquarters for the deputy supervisor who has charge of operations on government oil lands in California. His offices are in the Hopkins Building, at 19th and Chester Avenues.

At Bartlesville, Oklahoma, is the Petroleum Experiment Station, occupying a spacious two-story administration and petroleum laboratory building owned by the bureau and errected on land donated to the United States. The laboratory is fully equipped for conducting special investigations and for routine work. Equipment includes all apparatus necessary for making physical tests and chemical analyses of petroleum and petroleum products and also an experimental refinery. A complete machine shop and large garage form part of the station.

At Berkeley, California, the Pacific Mining Experiment Station, a mine-rescue station, and the headquarters of a district mining engineer are housed in the Hearst Memorial Mining Building of the University of California. The rescue station is supplied with a motor rescue-truck, and the university metallurgical laboratory equipment is used for experimental work.

At Birmingham, Alabama, the bureau owns a special building on land donated for the headquarters of a district mining engineer and for a mine-rescue station, which is equipped with a training gallery and a motor rescue-truck.

Under a coöperative agreement with the State of Colorado, offices and laboratories for study of oil shale problems are maintained at the University of Colorado, Boulder, Colorado.

Butte, Montana, is the headquarters of mine-rescue car No. 5.

Offices are maintained for a deputy oil and gas supervisor and his assistant at 508 Consolidated Royalty Company Building, Caspar, Wyoming. From this office, field work is directed and royalties are determined on government oil lands in Wyoming.

The Ceramics Experiment Station at Columbus, Ohio, is housed in Lord Hall, one of the buildings of Ohio State University. There are eight laboratories and a large gas-fired test kiln. Much of the equipment is specially designed to suit particular investigations.

The Dallas, Texas, field office for the study of petroleum production problems is located in the Insurance Building in quarters provided by the local chamber of commerce.

Denver, Colorado, is the headquarters for a district mining engineer, for the Mining Supervisor in charge of enforcement of the coal mine regulations under the act of February 25, 1920, as well as the Chief Oil and Gas Supervisor. These offices are all situated in the Custom House Building at Denver.

Des Moines, Iowa, is the headquarters of mine-rescue car No. 7.

A mine-rescue station, with a motor rescue-truck is maintained at Evansville, Indiana. The station is housed in the Post Office Building.

The Alaska Mining Experiment Station is at Fairbanks, and maintains an ore-testing laboratory and a chemical and assay laboratory in rented quarters.

Mine-rescue car No. 8 has headquarters at Huntington, West Virginia.

No. 10, a new steel car, is stationed at Ironwood, Michigan.

The Ithaca, New York., field office, which is concerned chiefly with problems in preparing special alloys and electric furnace practice, is located in one of the buildings of Cornell University. Some of the special laboratory equipment is owned by the bureau.

PLANT AND EQUIPMENT

At Knoxville, Tennessee, is a mine-rescue station, in the Post Office Building.

McAlester, Oklahoma, is a district headquarters of the Mining Division. There is a substantial brick mine-rescue station owned by the United States, equipped with a training gallery.

The offices of the North Central Mining Experiment Station are located at Minneapolis in a building provided by the University of Minnesota, and the laboratories of the School of Mines are available. One of these offices is also the headquarters of the district mining engineer.

The Moscow, Idaho, field office for investigation of ore treatment problems is housed in the School of Mines of the University of Idaho.

At Norton, Virginia, in the government building is a mine-rescue station.

The bureau maintains an office at Petrolia, Texas, in connection with its supervision of the helium plant, under funds supplied by the Army and Navy.

Pittsburgh, Kansas, is the headquarters of mine-rescue car No. 4.

The most important field post of the bureau is at Pittsburgh, Pennsylvania. Here is the headquarters of the Division of Mine-Rescue Cars and Stations, a district headquarters of the Mining Division, a mining experiment station, fuel testing laboratories, mine gas and coal analysis laboratories, explosives laboratory and general mining library, drafting, photography, and other service work, a mine-rescue station, equipped with a training gallery and a motor truck, and the headquarters of mine-rescue car No. 3. There is a series of new brick buildings, owned by the government and built on government land at 4800 Forbes Street. The main building is three stories high, has a frontage of 332 feet, and is flanked at either end with two-story wings, 45 by 211 feet. The central part of the building contains the administration offices. In the east wing are the chemical laboratories and in the west wing the mechanical laboratory. In the rear is a separate building occupied by the power plant and the metallurgical and fuel testing laboratories.

The experimental mine is located about a mile south of Bruceton, Pennsylvania, on land leased from a coal company. The mine has two parallel entries about 1400 feet long with three butt entries to one of the main entries; also rooms opening from these butt entries. There is a building for office work and for the storage of instruments; also a power plant and a grinding plant. Adjacent is the explosives testing station, where the safety and efficiency of various commercial explosives are determined for mine work.

Mine-rescue car No. 2 has headquarters at Raton, New Mexico.

Car No. 1, has headquarters at Reno, Nevada, where the Rare and Precious Metals Experiment Station is also situated in buildings owned by the University of Nevada.

Car No II is stationed at Rock Springs, Wyoming.

At Rolla, Missouri, in quarters furnished by the State School of Mines is the laboratory of the St. Louis Mining Experiment Station.

The St. Louis Mining Experiment Station is located in the Chamber of Commerce Building.

Salt Lake, Utah, is headquarters of a district mining engineer. The Intermountain Mining Experiment Station is quartered in buildings and laboratories provided by the University of Utah.

The San Francisco field office has offices in the Custom House and a laboratory equipped for research in petroleum problems.

At Seattle, Washington, is the Northwest Mining Experiment Station, and a mine-rescue station equipped with a training gallery and motor rescue-truck. Quarters are provided by the University of Washington.

The Shreveport field office for the supervision of leasing regulations in Louisiana fields is located in rented quarters at 614 Merchants Buildings, Shreveport, La.

PLANT AND EQUIPMENT

A new steel mine-rescue car, No. 9, has headquarters at Terre Haute, Indiana.

The laboratories of the Southern Mining Experiment Station are situated at Tuscaloosa, Ala., in quarters furnished by the University of Alabama, but for convenience in field work the head office is at Birmingham.

The Southwest Mining Experiment Station, at Tucson, Arizona, is housed in buildings and laboratories belonging to the University of Arizona.

At Vincennes, Indiana, is a mine-rescue station, housed in rented quarters in the La Plant building, and equipped with a rescue-truck. The district mining engineer also has his headquarters at this place.

The Central District Mining Experiment Station, situated at Urbana, Illinois, occupies quarters and uses laboratories provided by the University of Illinois.

A deputy oil and gas supervisor has been stationed at Winnett, Montana, with rented offices in a business building.

APPENDIX 5.

LAWS

(A) Index to Laws

Organization
Bureau of Mines established .... 36 Stat. L., 369
                                             37 Stat. L., 681

Personnel
Director, qualifications; appointment; salary .. 37 Stat. L., 681
Acting Director, Assistant Director or officer 39 Stat. L., 262,
    designated by Secretary 303
Federal Mine Inspector for Alaska, qualifica- 26 Stat. L., 1104
    tions; appointments; surety ....
———— Qualifications .... 36 Stat. L., 1363,
                                             1419
———— Salary; per diem and expenses ...... [a] 36 Stat. L.,
                                             703, 742
                                          [b] 41 Stat. L.,
                                             1367, 1401
———— Clerk for, salary; per diem and ex- [a] 38 Stat. L.,
    penses 822, 858
                                          [b] 41 Stat. L.,
                                             1367, 1401
Experts and other employees; appointment .... 37 Stat. L., 681
———— Field employees on temporary detail [a] 38 Stat. L.,
    to D. C. 822, 859
                                          [b] 41 Stat. L.,
                                             1367, 1402
———— Temporary, appointment; compensa- 37 Stat. L., 681,
    tion 682
———— At Washington, estimates required .. [a] 38 Stat. L.,
                                             609, 647
                                          [b] 41 Stat. L.,
                                             1367, 1402
General, no personal interest in subject of in- 37 Stat. L., 681,
    vestigations; no outside compensation for 682
    official services; no unofficial reports on prop-
    erty valuations ....
———— Limitation on personal service in D. [a] 38 Stat. L., 4,
    C. 48
                                          [b] 41 Stat. L.,
                                             1367, 1402

[a] Initial provision in act of appropriation which, being temporary, is reproduced in succeeding pages only in special cases.
[b] Current appropriation act, 1921-1922.

LAWS 83

Medical officers, may be detailed from Public Health Service .... [a] 40 Stat. L., 105, 146
[b] 41 Stat. L., 1367, 1402

Activities
Mine accidents, investigation .... [a] 36 Stat. L., 703, 742
37 Stat. L., 681
[b] 41 Stat. L., 1367, 1400
Mine-rescue stations, additional .... 38 Stat. L., 959
Mine-rescue cars, additional .... 38 Stat. L., 959
[a] 39 Stat. L., 262, 303
Mining, treatment, and utilization of minerals, investigation .... 37 Stat. L., 681
[a] 37 Stat. L., 417, 458
Mining, treatment, and utilization of nonmetallic minerals, investigation .... [b] 41 Stat. L., 1367, 1400
Pub. No. 18, 67 Cong.
Fuels, testing .... 37 Stat. L., 681
[a] 36 Stat. L., 703, 742
[b] 41 Stat. L., 1367, 1400
Peat, investigation .... 37 Stat. L., 681
Lignite and peat, investigation .... 40 Stat. L., 1154
Petroleum and natural gas, investigation ...... 37 Stat. L., 681
[a] 38 Stat. L., 609, 647
[b] 41 Stat. L., 1367, 1401
Mining experiment stations, additional .... 38 Stat. L., 959
[a] 39 Stat. L., 262, 302
[b] 41 Stat. L., 1367, 1401
Mines in Alaska, inspection .... 26 Stat. L., 1104
Mineral land leasing act, enforcement .... [a] 36 Stat. L., 703, 742
[b] 41 Stat. L., 1367, 1401
41 Stat. L., 437
[a] 41 Stat. L., 1156, 1172
[b] 41 Stat. L., 1367, 1401
Explosives, regulation   40 Stat. L., 385

[a] Initial provision in act of appropriation which, being temporary, is reproduced in succeeding pages only in special cases.
[b] Current appropriation act, 1921-1922.

Explosives, coöperation with Interstate Commerce Commission .... [a]40 Stat. L., 634, 671
41 Stat. L., 1444, 1445
War materials, investigation .... 40 Stat. L., 490
40 Stat. L., 1009, 1010
Government Fuel Yard, Washington, operation .. [a]40 Stat. L., 634, 673
41 Stat. L., 1367, 1402
War minerals relief, administration .... 40 Stat. L., 1272, 1274

Publications
Director to prepare and publish reports of inquiries and investigations .... 37 Stat. L., 681
[a]36 Stat. L., 703, 742
First editions limited; reprints authorized .... 36 Stat. L., 883

Plant
Land for mining experiment and mine-rescue stations, donations may be accepted ...... 38 Stat. L., 959
Land for mine-rescue car headquarters, purchase or lease; donations may be accepted ...... [a]37 Stat. L., 417, 458
Land for mining experiment station, Pittsburgh, Pa., may be accepted from city on exchange .... 39 Stat. L., 388
Land and building for mine-rescue stations, McAlester, Okla, purchase .... 38 Stat. L., 510
Land, etc., for Government Fuel Yard, Washington, purchase or lease .... 40 Stat. L., 634, 672
Building for mining experiment station, Pittsburgh, Pa., construction .... 37 Stat. L., 866, 888
Garage, mine-rescue station, Norton, Va. .... 38 Stat. L., 251
38 Stat. L., 609, 613
38 Stat. L., 822, 827
41 Stat. L., 1367, 1400
Building for headquarters, Washington, construction .... 36 Stat. L., 676, 699
37 Stat. L., 866, 880
Mine-rescue cars, additional, purchase .... 39 Stat. L., 262, 303
40 Stat. L., 105, 147

Appropriations
Estimates for personal service in D. C. required. [a]38 Stat. L., 609, 647
[b]41 Stat. L., 1367, 1402,

[a] Initial provision in act of appropriation which, being temporary, is reported in succeeding pages only in special cases.
[b] Current appropriation act, 1921-1922.

LAWS

Transfer of investigation appropriations by other [a] 41 Stat. L., 874, 913
branches of government authorized
[b] 41 Stat. L., 1367, 1402

Repayments
Sales of fuel, Government Fuel Yard; to "operation" .... [a] 40 Stat. L., 634, 673
[b] 41 Stat. L., 1367, 1402
Hauling services, Government Fuel Yard 41 Stat. L., 874, 913

Receipts, Miscellaneous
Fees for tests and investigations for private parties; to "miscellaneous receipts," Treasury [a] 36 Stat. L., 1363, 1419 .. 37 Stat. L., 681, 682

Expenditures
Supply and equipment, purchase on open market outside D. C. authorized; maximum $50 .... 40 Stat. L., 634, 672

(B) Compilation of Laws

1891—Act of March 3, 1891 (26 Stat. L., 1104)—An Act For the protection of the lives of miners in the Territories, as amended by the Act of July 1, 1902 (32 Stat. L., 631).[1]

[Sec. 1]. That in each organized and unorganized Territory of the United States wherein are located coal mines, the aggregate annual output of which shall be in excess of one thousand tons per annum, the President shall appoint a mine inspector, who shall hold office until his successor is appointed and qualified. Such inspector shall, before entering upon the discharge of his duties, give bond to the United States in the sum of two thousand dollars, conditioned for the faithful discharge of his duties.

Sec. 2. That no person shall be eligible for appointment as mine inspector under section one of this act who, is not either a practical miner or mining engineer and who has not been a resident for at least six months in the Territory for which he shall be appointed; and no person who shall act as land agent, manager, or agent of any mine, or as mining engineer, or be interested in operating any mine in such Territory shall be at the same time an inspector under the provisions of this act.

Sec. 3. That it shall be the duty of the mine inspector provided for in this act to make careful and thorough inspection of each coal mine operated in such Territory, and to report at least annually upon the condition of each coal mine in said Territory with reference to the appliances for the safety of the miners, the number of air or ventilating shafts, the number of shafts or slopes for ingress or egress, the character and condition of the machinery for ventilat-

---

[a] Initial provision in act of appropriation which, being temporary, is reported in succeeding pages only in special cases.
[b] Current appropriation act, 1921-1922.
[1] See Acts of June 25, 1910 and March 4, 1911

ing such mines, and the quantity of air supplied to same. Such report shall be made to the governor of the Territory in which such mines are located and a duplicate thereof forwarded to the Secretary of the Interior, and in the case of an unorganized Territory directly to the Secretary of the Interior.

Sec. 4. That in case the said mine inspector shall report that any coal mine is not properly constructed or not furnished with reasonable and proper machinery and appliances for the safety of the miners and other employees it shall be the duty of the governor of such organized Territory it shall be the duty [*sic*] of the Secretary of the Interior to give notice to the owners and managers of said coal mine that the said mine is unsafe and notifying them in what particular the same is unsafe, and requiring them to furnish or provide such additional machinery, slopes, entries, means of escape, ventilation, or other appliances necessary to the safety of the miners and other employees within a period to be in said notice named, and if the same be not furnished as required in such notice it shall be unlawful after the time fixed in such notice for the said owners or managers to operate said mine.

Sec. 5. That in all coal mines in the Territories of the United States the owners or managers shall provide at least two shafts, slopes, or other outlets, separated by natural strata or not less than one hundred and fifty feet in breadth, by which shafts, slopes, or outlets distinct means of ingress and egress shall always be available to the persons employed in said mine. And in case of the failure of any coal mine to be so provided it shall be the duty of the mine inspector to make report of such fact, and thereupon notice shall issue, as provided in section four of this act, and with the same force and effect.

Sec. 6. That the owners or managers of every coal mine shall provide an adequate amount of ventilation of not less than eighty-three and one-third cubic feet of pure air per second, or *five thousand* cubic feet per minute for every fifty men at work in said mine, and in like proportion for a greater number, which air shall by proper appliances or machinery be forced through such mine to the face of each and every working place, so as to dilute and render harmless and expel therefrom the noxious or poisonous gases. Wherever it is practicable to do so the entries, rooms, and all openings being operated in coal mines shall be kept well dampened with water to cause the coal dust to settle, and that when water is not obtainable at reasonable cost for this purpose accumulations of dust shall be taken out of the mine, and shall not be deposited in way places in the mine where it would be again distributed in the atmosphere by the ventilating currents. . . . [Italicized as amended.]

Sec. 7. That any mine owner or manager who shall continue to operate a mine after failure to comply with the requirements of this act and after the expiration of the period named in the notice provided for in section four of this act, shall be deemed guilty of a misdemeanor, and shall be fined not to exceed five hundred dollars.

Sec. 8. That in no case shall a furnace shaft be used or for the purposes of this act be deemed an escape shaft.

Sec. 9. That escape shafts shall be constructed in compliance with the requirements of this act within six months from the date of the passage hereof, unless the time shall be extended by the mine inspector, and in no case shall said time be extended to exceed one year from the passage of this act.

Sec. 10. That a metal speaking-tube from the top to the bottom of the shaft or slope shall be provided in all cases, so that conversation may be carried on through the same.

Sec. 11. That an approved safety catch shall be provided and sufficient cover overhead on every carriage used in lowering or hoisting persons. And the mine inspectors shall examine and pass upon the adequacy and safety of all such hoisting apparatus.

Sec. 12. That no child under twelve years of age shall be employed in the underground workings of any mine. And no father or other person shall misrepresent the age of anybody so employed. Any person guilty of violating the provisions of this section shall be deemed guilty of a misdemeanor, and upon conviction thereof shall be fined not to exceed one hundred dollars.

Sec. 13. That only experienced and competent and sober men shall be placed in charge of hoisting apparatus or engines. And the maximum number of persons who may ascend or descend upon any cage or hoisting apparatus shall be determined by the mine inspector.

Sec. 14. That it shall be lawful for any inspector to enter and inspect any coal mine in his district and the work and machinery belonging thereto at all reasonable times, but so as not to impede or obstruct the working of the mine; and to make inquiry into the state of the mine, works, and machinery, and the ventilation and mode of lighting the same, and into all matters and things connected with or relating to the safety of the persons employed in or about the same, and especially to make inquiry whether the provisions of this act are complied with; and the owner or agent is hereby required to furnish means necessary for such entry, inspection, examination and inquiry, of which the said inspector shall make an entry in the record in his office, noting the time and material circumstances of the inspection.

Sec. 15. That in all cases of fatal accident a full report thereof shall be made by the mine owner or manager to the mine inspector, said report to be in the [sic] writing and made within ten days after such deaths shall have occurred.

Sec. 16. That as a cumulative remedy, in case of the failure of any owner or manager of any mine to comply with the requirements contained in the notice of the Governor of such Territory or the Secretary of the Interior, given in pursuance of this act, any court of competent jurisdiction, or the judge of such court in vacation, may, on the application of the mine inspector in the name of the United States and supported by the recommendation of the governor of said Territory, or of the Secretary of the Interior, issue an injunction restraining the further operation of such mine until such requirements are complied with, and in order to obtain such injunction no bond shall be required.

Sec. 17. That wherever the term "owner or manager" is used in this act the same shall include lessees or other persons controlling the operation of any mine. And in case of the violation of the provisions of this act by any corporation the managing officers and superintendents, and other managing agents of such corporation, shall be personally liable and shall be punished as provided in act for owners and managers.

Sec. 18. That the mine inspectors provided for in this act shall each receive a salary of two thousand dollars per annum, and their actual travelling expenses when engaged in their duties. [See act of June 5, 1920.]

Sec. 19. That whenever any organized Territory shall make or has made provision by law for the safe operation of mines within such Territory, and the governor of such Territory shall certify said fact with a copy of the said law to the Secretary of the Interior, then and thereafter the provisions of this act shall no longer be enforced in such organized Territory, but in lieu thereof the statute of such Territory shall be operative in lieu of this act.

1910—Act of May 16, 1910 (36 Stat L., 369)—An Act To establish in the Department of the Interior a Bureau of Mines.[1]

Sec. 1. That there is hereby established in the Department of the Interior a bureau, to be called the Bureau of Mines, and a director of said bureau, who shall be thoroughly equipped for the duties of said office by technical education and experience and who shall be appointed by the President, by and with the advice and consent of the Senate, and who shall receive a salary of six thousand dollars per annum; and there shall also be in the said bureau such experts and other employees as may from time to time be authorized by Congress.

Sec. 2. That it shall be the province and duty of said bureau and its director, under the direction of the Secretary of the Interior, to make diligent investigations of the methods of mining, especially in relation to the safety of miners, and the appliances best adapted to prevent accidents, the possible improvement of conditions under which mining operations are carried on, the treatment of ores and other mineral substances, the use of explosives and electricity, the prevention of accidents, and other inquiries and technologic investigations pertinent to said industries, and from time to time make such public reports of the work, investigations, and information obtained as the Secretary of the said department may direct, with the recommendations of such bureau.

Sec. 3. That the Secretary of the Interior shall provide the said bureau with furnished offices in the city of Washington, with such books, records, stationery and appliances, and such assistants, clerks, stenographers, typewriters, and other employees as may be necessary for the proper discharge of the duties imposed by this Act upon such bureau, fixing the compensation of such clerks and employees within appropriations made for that purpose.

[1] The original organic act; amended and superseded by the act of February 25, 1913.

LAWS

Sec. 4. That the Secretary of the Interior is hereby authorized to transfer to the Bureau of Mines from the United States Geological Survey the supervision of the investigations of structural materials and the analyzing and testing of coals, lignites, and other mineral fuel substances and the investigation as to the causes of mine explosions; and the appropriations made for such investigations may be expended under the supervision of the Director of the Bureau of Mines in manner as if the same were so directed in the appropriations Acts; and such investigations shall hereafter be within the province of the Bureau of Mines, and shall cease and determine under the organization of the United States Geological Survey; and such experts, employees, property and equipment as are now employed or used by the Geological Survey in connection with the subjects herewith transferred to the Bureau of Mines are directed to be transferred to said bureau. [Repealed by act of June 25, 1910, in so far as it relates to the transfer to the Bureau of Mines of the supervision of the inspection of structural materials and equipment.]

Sec. 5. That nothing in this Act shall be construed as in any way granting to any officer or employee of the Bureau of Mines any right or authority in connection with the inspection or supervision of mines or metallurgical plants in any State.

Sec 6. This Act shall take effect and be in force on and after the first day of July, nineteen hundred and ten.

1910—Act of June 25, 1910 (36 Stat L., 676, 699)—An Act To increase the limit of cost of certain public buildings, to authorize the enlargement, extension, remodeling or improvement of certain public buildings, to authorize the erection and completion of public buildings, to authorize the purchase of sites for public buildings, and for other purposes.

* * * *

Sec. 32. That the Secretary of the Treasury be, and he is hereby, authorized and directed to prepare designs and estimates for a fireproof building of modern office-building type of architecture to be erected on square numbered one hundred and forty-three, in the City of Washington, District of Columbia, now owned by the United States, which building, including fireproof vaults, heating and ventilating apparatus, elevators, and approaches, complete, to cost not exceeding two million five hundred thousand dollars, and to be designed and constructed of sufficient area and capacity to occupy all of said square as a building site, and to afford, when completed, office accommodations for the entire organization at Washington of the office of the Geological Survey, office of Indian Affairs, office of the Reclamation Service, the General Land Office, and the Bureau of Mines; and such designs and estimates shall be approved by a board consisting of the Secretary of the Interior, the Secretary of the Treasury, and the Superintendent of the Capitol Buildings and Grounds: *Provided,* That no part of the amount heretofore mentioned as the limit of cost is authorized to be appropriated by this Act except for the preparation of designs and estimates. And so much as may be necessary of the unexpended balance of the amount heretofore authorized for the acquisition of said site shall be available for the preparation of designs and estimates: *Provided further,* That the foregoing authorization shall be in addition to and independent of the authorizations and appropriations for personal services for the office of the Supervising Architect otherwise made.

1910—Act of June 25, 1910 (36 Stat. L., 703, 742, 743)— An Act Making appropriations for sundry civil expenses of the Government for the fiscal year ending June thirtieth, nineteen hundred and twelve, and for other purposes.

* * * *

Said inspectors [authorized by the act of March 3, 1891] are hereby authorized to inspect coal and other mines in the District of Alaska, to which District the provisions of said act are hereby extended and made applicable.

* * * *

So much of the act establishing a Bureau of Mines, approved May sixteenth, nineteen hundred and ten, as transfers to said Bureau the supervision of the investigations of structural materials and equipment therefor is repealed.

1910—Joint Resolution of June 25, 1910 (36 Stat. L., 883)— Joint Resolution Limiting the editions of the publications of the Bureau of Mines.

[Sec. 1]. That the publications of the Bureau of Mines shall be published in such editions as recommended by the Secretary of the Interior, but not to exceed ten thousand copies for the first edition.

Sec. 2. That whenever the edition of any of the publications of the Bureau of Mines shall have become exhausted and the demand for it continues, there shall be published, on the requisition of the Secretary of the Interior, as many additional copies as the Secretary of the Interior may deem necessary to meet the demand.

1911—Act of March 4, 1911 (36 Stat. L., 1363, 1419)—An Act Making appropriations for sundry civil expenses of the Government for the fiscal year ending June thirtieth, nineteen hundred and twelve, and for other purposes.

LAWS

* * * *

For tests or investigations authorized by the Secretary of the Interior, other than those performed for the Government of the United States, a reasonable fee covering actual necessary expenses shall be charged, according to a schedule submitted by the director and approved by the Secretary of the Interior, who shall prescribe the rules and regulations under which such tests or investigations shall be made and under which such fees shall be charged and collected. All moneys received from such fees shall be paid into the Treasury to the credit of miscellaneous receipts;

* * * *

Said inspectors [authorized by the act of March 3, 1891] are hereby authorized to inspect coal and other mines in the District of Alaska, to which District the provisions of said Act, except so much as requires six months residence in a Territory prior to appointment, are hereby extended and made applicable.

1912—Act of August 24, 1912 (37 Stat. L., 417, 458—An Act Making appropriations for sundry civil expenses of the Government for the fiscal year ending June thirtieth, nineteen hundred and thirteen, and for other purposes.

* * * *

That no part thereof [appropriation "for inquiries and investigations into the mining and treatment of ores and other mineral substances, with special reference to safety and waste"] may be used for investigation in behalf of any private party, nor shall any part thereof be used for work authorized by law to be done by any other branch of the public service. [Repeated in act of June, 23, 1913, 38 Stat. L., 4, 48; act of August 1, 1914, 38 Stat. L., 609, 647; act of March 3, 1915, 38 Stat. L., 822, 858; and act of July 1, 1916, 39 Stat. L., 262, 302.]

* * * *

For the purchase or lease of the necessary land, where and under such conditions as the Secretary of the Interior may direct, for the headquarters of five mine-rescue cars and for the construction of the necessary railway sidings on the same, $4,000: *Provided,* That the Secretary of the Interior is hereby authorized to accept any suitable land or lands that may be donated for said purpose.

1913—Act of February 25, 1913 (37 Stat. L., 681)—An Act To amend an Act entitled "An Act to establish in the Department of the Interior a Bureau of Mines," approved May sixteenth, nineteen hundred and ten.

[Sec. 1]. That the Act to establish in the Department of the Interior a Bureau of Mines, approved May sixteenth, nineteen hundred

and ten, be, and the same is hereby, amended to read as follows:
"That there is hereby established in the Department of the Interior a bureau of mining, metallurgy, and mineral technology, to be designated the Bureau of Mines, and there shall be a director of said bureau, who shall be thoroughly equipped for the duties of said office by technical education and experience and who shall be appointed by the President, by and with the advice and consent of the Senate, and who shall receive a salary of six thousand dollars per annum; and there shall also be in the said bureau such experts and other employees, to be appointed by the Secrtary of the Interior, as may be required to carry out the purposes of this Act in accordance with the appropriations made from time to time by Congress for such purposes.

Sec. 2. That it shall be the province and duty of the Bureau of Mines, subject to the approval of the Secretary of the Interior, to conduct inquiries and scientific and technologic investigations concerning mining, and the preparation, treatment, and utilization of mineral substances with a view to improving health conditions, and increasing safety, efficiency, economic development, and conserving resources through the prevention of waste in the mining, quarrying, metallurgical, and other mineral industries; to inquire into the economic conditions affecting these industries; to investigate explosives and peat; and on behalf of the government to investigate the mineral fuels and unfinished mineral products belonging to, or for the use of, the United States, with a view to their most efficient mining, preparation, treatment and use; and to disseminate information concerning these subjects in such manner as will best carry out the purposes of this Act.

Sec. 3. That the director of said bureau shall prepare and publish, subject to the direction of the Secretary of the Interior, under the appropriations made from time to time by Congress, reports of inquiries and investigations, with appropriate recommendations of the bureau, concerning the nature, causes, and prevention of accidents, and the improvement of conditions, methods, and equipment, with special referenec to health, safety, and prevention of waste in the mining, quarrying, metallurgical, and other mineral industries; the use of explosives and electricity, safety methods and appliances, and rescue and first-aid work in said industries; the causes and prevention of mine fires; and other subjects included under the provisions of this Act.

Sec. 4. In conducting inquiries and investigations authorized by this Act neither the director nor any member of the Bureau of Mines shall have any personal or private interest in any mine or the products of any mine under investigation, or shall accept employment from any private party for services in the examination of any mine or private mineral property, or issue any report as to the valuation or the management of any mine or other private mineral property: *Provided,* That nothing herein shall be construed as preventing the temporary employment by the Bureau of Mines, at a compensation not to exceed ten dollars per day, in a consulting capacity or in the investigation of special subjects, of any engineer or other expert whose principal professional practice is outside of such employment by said bureau.

Sec. 5. That for tests or investigations authorized by the Secretary of the Interior under the provisions of this Act, other than those performed for the Government of the United States or State governments within the United States a reasonable fee covering the necessary expenses shall be charged, according to a schedule prepared by the Director of the Bureau of Mines and approved by the Secretary of the Interior, who shall prescribe rules and regulations under which such tests and investigations may be made. All moneys received from such sources shall be paid into the Treasury to the credit of miscellaneous receipts.

Sec. 6. That this Act shall take effect and be in force on and after its passage.

1913—Act of June 23, 1913 (38 Stat. L., 4, 48)—An Act Making appropriations for sundry civil expenses of the Government for the fiscal year ending June thirtieth, nineteen hundred and fourteen, and for other purposes.

* * * *

For the purchase or lease of the necessary land, where and under such conditions as the Secretary of the Interior may direct, for the headquarters of five mine-rescue cars and for the construction of the necessary railway sidings on the same, $2,000: *Provided,* That the Secretary of the Interior is hereby authorized to accept any suitable land or lands that may be donated for said purpose.

1913—Act of March 4, 1913 (37 Stat. L., 866, 880, 886)— An Act To increase the limit of cost of certain public buildings, to authorize the enlargement, extension, remodeling, or improvement of certain public buildings, to authorize the erection and completion of public buildings, to authorize the purchase of sites for public buildings, and for other purposes.

* * * *

Sec. 9. That the Secretary of the Treasury be, and he is hereby, authorized and directed to cause to be constructed on square numbered one hundred and forty-three, in the city of Washington, District of Columbia, a fireproof building of modern office building type of architecture of sufficient area to afford when completed office accommodations for the entire organization at Washington, District of Columbia, of the Geological Survey, Reclamation Service, Indian Office, Bureau of Mines, and such other offices and bureaus of the Interior Department as can be accommodated therein.

That the plans, specifications, and estimates for said building shall be approved by a board consisting of the Secretary of the

Treasury, the Secretary of the Interior, and the Superintendent of the Capitol Building and Grounds.

That for the purpose of beginning the construction of said building the sum of $596,000 is hereby authorized, and the unexpended balance of the appropriation for the acquisition of said square one hundred and forty-three is hereby made available as a part of said authorization for the employment, at customary rates of compensation without regard to civil-service laws, rules, or regulations, of technical and engineering services in the Office of the Supervising Architect, exclusively to aid in the preparation of the necessary plans, specifications, estimates, and toward the commencement of the construction of said building.

That the foregoing authorization for the employment of technical and engineering services shall be in addition to and independent of the authorizations and appropriations for personal services for the Office of the Supervising Architect otherwise made: *Provided,* That this authorization shall not be construed as fixing the limit of cost of said building at the sum hereby named, but the building hereby authorized shall be constructed or so planned as to cost, complete, including fireproof vaults, heating and ventilating apparatus, elevators, lighting fixtures, and approaches, but exclusive of site, not exceeding $2,596,000.

That the Secretary of the Treasury be, and he is hereby, authorized and directed to enter into contracts for the construction of a suitable building for said purpose within the ultimate limit of cost above mentioned.

* * * *

Sec. 26. That the Secretary of the Treasury be, and he is hereby, authorized and directed to enter into a contract or contracts for the erection and completion of fireproof laboratories and other buildings suitable and necessary for the investigations of the Bureau of Mines, on a site hereinafter provided, in the city of Pittsburgh, Pennsylvania, within the total limit of cost hereinafter fixed.

That the said laboratories and other buildings shall be constructed under the direction of and in accordance with plans and estimates to be approved by a board consisting of the Director of the Bureau of Mines, the Chief of Engineers of the Army, and the Supervising Architect of the Treasury, and shall be so constructed as to cost, complete, with the necessary railroad sidings approaches, plumbing, lighting, heating, ventilating and hoisting apparatus, and other necessary appurtenances, not to exceed the sum of $500,000, of which amount the sum of $250,000 is hereby authorized and shall be immediately available for the preparation of plans for said laboratories and other buildings and for carrying forward construction work. And the Secretary of the Treasury is hereby authorized to employ, without regard to civil-service laws, rules, or regulations and to pay for at customary rates of compensation, out of this authorization, such technical and engineering services as may be recommended by the above board, to serve exclusively in the Office of the Supervising Architect of the Treasury Department to aid in the preparation of plans and specifications for and to supervise the construction of the work herein provided for: *Provided,* That the foregoing authorization for the employment of technical and engineering services shall be in addition to and independent of the authorizations and appropriations for personal services for the Office of the Supervising Architect otherwise made.

That the Secretary of War be, and he is hereby, authorized to transfer to the city of Pittsburgh, Pennsylvania, or to the board of public education of the said city of Pittsburgh, for public use, that part of the United States arsenal grounds in the city of Pittsburgh lying between Thirty-ninth and Fortieth Streets and between Butler Street and the tract of land transferred by the Secretary of War to the custody and control of the Treasury Department for a marine-hospital site by an instrument dated June first, nineteen hundred and four, under authority of the sundry civil Act of March third, nineteen hundred and three, the land to be transferred to the said city of Pittsburgh being more particularly described as follows: Beginning at the northwest corner of the said tract of land transferred to the custody and control of the Treasury Department, and running thence along Fortieth Street in a northwesterly direction to the intersection of said street and Butler Street, one thousand one hundred and seventeen and one-half feet, more or less; thence along Butler Street in a southwesterly direction to the intersection of said street and Thirty-ninth Street, five hundred and twenty-three feet, more or less; thence along Thirty-ninth Street in a southwesterly direction to southwest corner of the said tract of land transferred to the custody and control of the Treasury Department, one thousand one hundred and one-half feet, more or less; and thence along the westerly boundary of said tract of land in a northeasterly direction to the place of beginning, five hundred and twenty-three feet, more or less; and containing thirteen and one-fourth acres, more or less, on the transfer by the board of public education of the city of Pittsburgh, or by the city of Pittsburgh to the United States, for the use of the Bureau of Mines, under the Department of the Interior, as a site for the erection of the laboratories and other buildings hereinbefore provided for, of the tract of land in the said city of Pittsburgh, known as the Magee High School site, and lying on Forbes Street and the Baltimore and Ohio Railroad, and more particularly described as follows: Beginning in the center of Boundary Street at its junction with Forbes Street and running north eighty-seven degrees thirty-six minutes forty-five seconds east parallel to Forbes Street for a distance of five hundred and thirty-six and two-tenths feet, more or less, to a stone monument; thence running south two degrees twenty-three minutes fifteen seconds east for a distance of one hundred and fifty feet, more or less, to a stone monument; thence north eighty-seven degrees thirty-six minutes forty-five seconds east for a distance of one hundred and fifteen feet, more or less, to a stone monument; thence north two degrees twenty-three-minutes fifteen seconds west for a distance of fifty-eight and eighty-nine one-hundredths feet, more or less, to a stone monument; thence south fifty-two degrees twenty-six minutes fifteen seconds east for a distance of twenty and eighty one-hundredths feet, more or less, to a pin; thence south fifty degrees forty-one minutes fifteen seconds east for a distance of four hundred and thirteen and eight-tenths feet, more or less, to a pin; thence south fifteen degrees twenty-eight minutes forty-five seconds west for a distance of three hundred and twenty-six and seventy one-hundredths feet, more or less, to a pin; thence north seventy-six degrees forty-five minutes west for a distance of one thousand one hundred and forty-four and seventy-five one-hundredths feet, more or less, to the center of Boundary Street, and thence along the center of Boundary Street north twenty-eight degrees fifteen minutes east for a distance of four hundred and forty-four and thirty-eight one-hundredths feet, more or less, to the starting point, and containing an area of eleven and one-half acres, more or less: *Provided,* That before the above-described transfer by the Secretary of War to the city of Pittsburgh shall become effective, and as an express further consideration for said transfer, and for the surrender by the United States of a perpetual water supply now obtained from a reservoir located on the lands so to be transferred, the city of Pittsburgh, through its proper officers, shall covenant and agree, at its own expense, and within a reasonable time, to tap, within that part of the Pittsburgh supply depot and reservation between Butler Street and the Allegheny River retained by the United States, the forty-two inch water main belonging to the said city which now crosses the said reservation under a revocable license, and thereafter to furnish, in perpetuity free of charge to the United States, all the water needed of good quality for said purposes for all purposes upon the said reservation, and shall also agree to keep its own water main, pipes, hydrants, and other necessary appurtenances now located or hereafter to be located upon the same, in good condition and repair at its own expense. In case of failure of the city of Pittsburgh to do any and all things necessary to proper fulfillment of this provision, the reservoir, pipe lines, and so much of the land adjacent thereto on the part of the reservation which is to be transferred to the said city as may be needed for rights of way shall revert to the United States. [Amended by act of December 22, 1913.]

1913—Act of December 22, 1913 (38 Stat. L., 251)—An Act Amending an Act entitled "An Act to increase the limit of cost of certain public buildings, to authorize the enlargement, extension, remodeling, or improvement of certain public buildings, to authorize the erection of certain public buildings, to authorize the erection and completion of public buildings, to authorize the purchase of sites for public buildings, and for other purposes," approved March fourth, nineteen hundred and thirteen.

That section twenty-six of the Act approved March fourth, nineteen hundred and thirteen, which authorizes the Secretary of the Treasury to enter into a contract or contracts for the erection of fireproof laboratories for the Bureau of Mines in the city of Pittsburgh, Pennsylvania, and so forth, is hereby amended so as to authorize the Secretary of the Treasury, in his discretion, to accept and expend, in addition to the limit of cost therein fixed, such funds as may be received by contribution from the State of Pennsylvania, or from other sources, for the purpose of enlarging, by purchase, condemnation, or otherwise, and improving the site authorized to be acquired for said Bureau of Mines, or for other work contemplated by said legislation: *Provided*, That the acceptance of such contributions and the improvements made therewith shall involve the United States in no expenditure in excess of the limit of cost heretofore fixed.

1914—Act of July 7, 1914 (38 Stat. L., 510)—An Act For the purchase of a building and lot as a mine rescue station at McAlester, Oklahoma.

That the Secretary of the Interior be, and he is hereby, authorized and directed to purchase, for and on behalf of the United States, the following-described real estate in the city of McAlester, county of Pittsburg, State of Oklahoma, to wit, the north fifty feet of lot numbered two, in block numbered four hundred and eighty-seven, in the original town site of South McAlester, the dimensions of said lot being fifty feet by one hundred and sixty-five feet, with fifty feet front to South Third Street, in said city of McAlester, together with the two-story brick building and all other improvements thereon, for the use of the Bureau of Mines for a mine rescue station and for such other purposes as the Bureau of Mines may from time to time desire to use the same, at and for the sum of $5,500, which said sum is hereby appropriated for such purchase out of any money in the Treasury not otherwise appropriated.

1914—Act of August 1, 1914 (38 Stat. L., 609, 613, 647)—An Act Making appropriations for sundry civil expenses of the Government for the fiscal year ending June thirtieth, nineteen hundred and fifteen, and for other purposes.

* * * *
Pittsburgh, Pennsylvania, Bureau of Mines: For technical services and for commencement of building, $150,000.
* * * *
For the fiscal year nineteen hundred and sixteen, and annually thereafter estimates shall be submitted specifically for all personal services required permanently and entirely in the Bureau of Mines at Washington, District of Columbia, and previously paid from lump sum or general appropriations. [Repeated in act of March 3, 1915; 38 Stat. L., 822, 858.]
* * * *

For the purchase or lease of the necessary land, where and under such conditions as the Secretary of the Interior may direct, for the headquarters of five mine-rescue cars and for the construction of the necessary railway sidings on the same, $1,000: *Provided,* That the Secretary of the Interior is authorized to accept any suitable land or lands that may be donated for said purpose.

1915—Act of March 3, 1915 (38 Stat. L., 822, 827, 859)—An Act Making appropriations for sundry civil expenses of the Government for the fiscal year ending June thirtieth, nineteen hundred and sixteen, and for other purposes.

* * * *

Pittsburgh, Pennsylvania, laboratories, Bureau of Mines: For completion, $350,000.

* * * *

For purchase or lease of necessary land, where and under such conditions as the Secretary of the Interior may direct, for the headquarters of mine-rescue cars and construction of necessary railway sidings on the same, $1,000: *Provided,* That the Secretary of the Interior is authorized to accept any suitable land or lands that may be donated for said purpose.

* * * *

Persons employed during the fiscal year nineteen hundred and sixteen in field work, outside of the District of Columbia, under the Bureau of Mines, may be detailed temporarily for service in Washington, District of Columbia, for purposes of preparing results of their field work; all persons so detailed shall be paid in addition to their regular compensation only their actual traveling expenses or per diem in lieu of subsistence in going to and returning therefrom: *Provided,* That nothing herein shall prevent the payment to employees of the Bureau of Mines their necessary expenses or per diem, in lieu of subsistence while on temporary detail in Washington, District of Columbia, for purposes only of consultation or investigations on behalf of the United States. All details made hereunder, and the purposes of each, during the preceding fiscal year, shall be reported in the annual estimates of appropriations to Congress at the beginning of each regular session thereof. [Repeated in act of July 1, 1916, 39 Stat. L., 262, 303; act of June 12, 1917, 40 Stat. L., 105, 147; act of July 1, 1918, 40 Stat. L., 634, 672; act of July 19, 1919, 40 Stat. L., 163, 199; and act of June 5, 1920, 41 Stat. L., 874, 912.]

1915—Act of March 3, 1915 (38 Stat. L., 959)—An Act To provide for the establishment and maintenance of mining and experiment and mine safety stations for making investigations and disseminating information among employees in mining, quarrying, metallurgical, and other mineral industries, and for other purposes.

[Sec. 1]. That the Secretary of the Interior is hereby authorized and directed to establish and maintain in the several important mining regions of the United States and the Territory of Alaska, as Congress may appropriate for the necessary employees and other expenses, under the Bureau of Mines and in accordance with the provision of the Act establishing said bureau, ten mining experiment stations and seven mine safety stations, movable or stationary, in addition to those already established, the province and duty of which shall be to make investigations and disseminate information with a view to improving conditions in the mining, quarrying, metallurgical, and other mineral industries, safeguarding life among employees, preventing unnecessary waste of resources, and otherwise contributing to the advancement of these industries: *Provided,* That not more than three mining experiment stations and mine safety stations hereinabove authorized shall be established in any one fiscal year under the appropriations made therefor.

Sec. 2. That the Secretary of the Interior is hereby authorized to accept lands, buildings, or other contributions from the several States offering to coöperate in carrying out the purposes of this Act.

1916—Act of July 1, 1916 (39 Stat. L., 262, 303)—An Act Making appropriations for sundry civil expenses of the Government for the fiscal year ending June thirtieth, nineteen hundred and seventeen, and for other purposes.

* * * *

For purchase of three additional mine-rescue cars, $53,000.

* * * *

For purchase or lease of necessary land, where and under such conditions as the Secretary of the Interior may direct, for the headquarters of mine rescue cars and construction of necessary railway sidings and housing for the same, or as the site of an experimental mine and a plant for studying explosives, $1,000. *Provided,* That the Secretary of the Interior is authorized to accept any suitable land or lands, buildings, or improvements, that may be donated for said purpose, and to enter into leases for periods not exceeding ten years, subject to annual appropriations by Congress.

* * * *

Hereafter in the absence of the Director of the Bureau of Mines the assistant director of said bureau shall perform the duties of the director during the latter's absence, and in the absence of the Director and of the Assistant Director of the Bureau of Mines the Secretary of the Interior may designate some officer of said bureau to perform the duties of the director during his absence.

1916—Joint Resolution of July 21, 1916 (39 Stat. L., 388)—
Joint Resolution To authorize the Secretary of the
Treasury to accept from the city of Pittsburgh certain
lands in exchange for other lands of equal area.

That the Secretary of the Treasury be, and he is hereby, authorized to accept from the city of Pittsburgh, State of Pennsylvania, that certain lot or parcel of land bounded and described as follows:

Beginning at a point on the line dividing the properties owned by the city of Pittsburgh and the United States of America, occupied by the Bureau of Mines, at a point north seventy-six degrees forty-five minutes west forty-two and eight-tenths feet from the southeast corner of the said property of the United States of America; thence south fifteen degrees twenty-four minutes fifty-five seconds west four hundred and six one-hundredths feet to a point; thence north seventy-four degrees thirty-six minutes fifty-five seconds west eighteen and forty-four one-hundredths feet to a point; thence south fifteen degrees twenty-eight minutes forty-five seconds west thirty-seven and eighty-seven one-thousandths feet to a point; thence north seventy-four degrees thirty-six minutes fifty-five seconds west four hundred and forty-nine and sixty-six one-hundredths feet to a point; thence north fifteen degrees twenty-eight minutes forty-five seconds east twenty-one and seven hundred and twenty-seven one-thousandths feet to a point on the said line dividing the properties of the city of Pittsburgh and the United States of America; thence south seventy-six degrees forty-five minutes east nine hundred and seven and thirty-nine one-hundredths feet to the place of beginning, containing eighteen thousand square feet, more or less, for the use of the Bureau of Mines of the Department of the Interior, and to transfer to the city of Pittsburgh in exchange therefor that certain lot or parcel of land now constituting a part of the grounds of the Bureau of Mines of the Department of the Interior bounded and described as follows:

Beginning at a point on the line dividing the properties owned by the city of Pittsburgh and the United States of America, occupied by the Bureau of Mines, at a point north seventy-six degrees forty-five minutes west forty-two and eight-tenths feet from the southeast corner of said property of the United States of America; thence north fifteen degrees twenty-four minutes fifty-five seconds east three hundred and forty-seven and eight-tenths feet to a point on the dividing line between the properties of the United States of America and the Carnegie Institute of Technology, a Pennsylvania corporation; thence along said dividing line south fifty degrees forty-one minutes fifteen seconds east forty-seven and eighteen one-hundredths feet to a point; thence along the line dividing the property of the United States of America from the property of the said Carnegie Institute of Technology and the city of Pittsburgh south fifteen degrees twenty-eight minutes forty-five seconds west three hundred and twenty-seven and eight one-hundredths feet to a point; thence north seventy-six degrees forty-five minutes west forty-two and eight-tenths feet to the place of beginning; together with that part of a circular tract lying west of the above-described tract of land and included within an arc struck with a radius of fifty-one feet from a point five feet east of a point on the westerly line two hundred and fifty-seven feet from the southwest corner of the above-described tract; said lot or parcel of ground comprising eighteen thousand square feet, more or less.

1917—Act of June 12, 1917 (40 Stat. L., 105, 146)—An Act Making appropriations for sundry civil expenses of the Government for the fiscal year ending June thirtieth, nineteen hundred and eighteen, and for other purposes.

* * * *

That no part thereof [appropration "for inquiries and scientific and technologic investigations concerning the mining, preparation, treatment, and utilization of ores and other mineral substances" and "the economic conditions affecting these industries"] may be used in behalf of any private party. [Repeated in act of July 1, 1918, 40 Stat. L., 634, 670; act of July 19, 1919, 41 Stat. L., 163, 198; and act of June 5, 1920, 41 Stat. L., 874, 911.]

* * * *

The Secretary of the Treasury may detail medical officers of the Public Health Service for coöperative health, safety, or sanitation work with the Bureau of Mines, and the compensation and expenses of officers so detailed may be paid from the applicable appropriations made herein for the Bureau of Mines. [Repeated in act of July 1, 1918, 40 Stat. L., 634, 671; act of July 19, 1919, 41 Stat. L., 163, 199; and act of June 5, 1920, 41 Stat. L., 874, 911.]

* * * *

For purchase of three additional mine-rescue cars, $81,750.

* * * *

For purchase or lease of necessary land, where and under such conditions as the Secretary of the Interior may direct, for the headquarters of mine-rescue cars and construction of necessary railway sidings and housing for the same, or as the site of an experimental mine and a plant for studying explosives, $1,000: *Provided,* That the Secretary of the Interior is authorized to accept any suitable land or lands, buildings, or improvements, that may be donated for said purpose and to enter into leases for periods not exceeding ten years, subject to annual appropriations by Congress.

1917—Act of October 6, 1917 (40 Stat. L., 385)—An Act To prohibit the manufacture, distribution, storage, use, and possession in time of war of explosives, providing regulations for the safe manufacture, dis-

distribution, storage, use, and possession of the same, and for other purposes.

[Sec. 1]. That when the United States is at war [1] it shall be unlawful to manufacture, distribute, store, use, or possess powder, explosives, blasting supplies, or ingredients thereof, in such manner as to be detrimental to the public safety, except as in this Act provided.

Sec. 2. That the words "explosive" and "explosives" when used herein shall mean gunpowders, powders used for blasting, all forms of high explosives, blasting materials, fuses, detonators, and other detonating agents, smokeless powders, and any chemical compound or mechanical mixture that contains any oxidizing and combustibe units or other ingredients in such proportions, quantities or packing that ignition by fire, by friction, by concussion, by percussion, or by detonation of, or any part of, the compound or mixture may cause such a sudden generation of highly heated gases that the resultant gaseous pressures are capable of producing destructive effects on contiguous objects, or of destroying life or limb, but shall not include small arms or shotgun cartridges: *Provided,* That nothing herein contained shall be construed to prevent the manufacture, under the authority of the Government, of explosives for, their sale to or their possession by, the military or naval service of the United States of America.

Sec. 3. That the word "ingredients" when used herein shall mean the materials and substances capable by combination of producing one or more of the explosives mentioned in section one hereof.

Sec. 4. That the word "person," when used herein, shall include States, Territories, the District of Columbia, Alaska, and other dependencies of the United (States, and municipal subdivisions thereof, individual citizens, firms, assocations, societies and corporations of the United States and of other countries at peace with the United States.

Sec. 5. That from and after forty days after the passage and approval of this Act no person shall have in his possession or purchase, accept, receive, sell, give, barter or otherwise dispose of or procure explosives, or ingredients, except as provided in this Act: *Provided,* That the purchase or possession of said ingredients when purchased or held in small quantities and not used or intended to be used in the manufacture of explosives are not subject to the provisions of this Act: *Provided further,* That the superintendent, foreman, or other duly authorized employee, at a mine, quarry, or other work, may, when licensed so to do, sell or issue, to any workman under him, such an amount of explosives, or ingredients, as may be required by that workman in the performance of his duties, and the workman may purchase or accept the explosives, or ingredients, so sold or issued, but the person so selling or issuing same shall see that any unused explosives, or ingredients, are returned, and that no explosives, or ingredients, are taken by the workman to any point not necessary to the carrying on of his duties.

[1] Expired March 3, 1921.—Jt. Res. of March 3, 1921; 41 Stat. L., 1359.

Sec. 6. That nothing contained herein shall apply to explosives or ingredients while being transported upon vessels or railroad cars in conformity with statutory law or Interstate Commerce Commission rules.

Sec. 7. That from and after forty days after the passage of this Act no person shall manufacture explosives unless licensed so to do, as hereinafter provided.

Sec. 8. That any licensee or applicant for license hereunder shall furnish such information regarding himself and his business, so far as such business relates to or is connected with explosives or ingredients at such time and in such manner as the Director of the Bureau of Mines, or his authorized representative, may request, excepting that those who have been or are at the time of the passage of this Act regularly engaged in the manufacture of explosives shall not be compelled to disclose secret processes, costs, or other data unrelated to the distribution of explosives.

Sec. 9. That from and after forty days after the passage and approval of this Act every person authorized to sell, issue, or dispose of explosives shall keep a complete itemized and accurate record, showing each person to whom explosives are sold, given, bartered, or to whom or how otherwise disposed of, and the quantity and kind of explosives, and the date of each such sale, gift, barter, or other disposition; and this record shall be sworn to and furnished to the Director of the Bureau of Mines, or his authorized representatives, whenever requested.

Sec. 10. That the Director of the Bureau of Mines is hereby authorized to issue licenses as follows:

(*a*) Manufacturer's license, authorizing the manufacture, possession, and sale of explosives and ingredients.

(*b*) Vendor's license, authorizing the purchase, possession, and sale of explosives or ingredients.

(*c*) Purchaser's license, authorizing the purchase and possession of explosives and ingredients.

(*d*) Foreman's license, authorizing the purchase and possession of explosives and ingredients, and the sale and issuance of explosives and ingredients to workmen under the proviso to section five above.

(*e*) Exporters' license, authorizing the licensee to export explosives, but no such license shall authorize exportation in violation of any proclamation of the President issued under any Act of Congress.

(*f*) Importer's license, authorizing the licensee to import explosives.

(*g*) Analyst's, educator's, inventor's, and investigator's licenses authorizing the purchase, manufacture, possession, testing, and disposal of explosives and ingredients.

Sec. 11. That the Director of the Bureau of Mines shall issue licenses, upon application duly made, but only to citizens of the United States of America, and to the subjects or citizens of nations that are at peace with them, and to corporations, firms, and associations thereof, and he may, in his discretion, refuse to issue a license when he has reason to believe from facts of which he has knowledge or reliable information, that the applicant is disloyal or hostile to the United States of America, or that, if the applicant is a firm, association, society, or corporation, its controlling stockholders or members are disloyal or hostile to the United States of America. The director may, when he has reason to believe on like grounds that any licensee is so disloyal or hostile, revoke any license issued to him. Any applicant to whom a license is refused or any licensee whose license is revoked by the said director, may, at any time within thirty days after notification of the rejection of his application or revocation of his license, apply for such license or the cancellation of such revocation to the Council of National Defense, which shall make its order upon the director either to grant or to withhold the license.

Sec. 12. That any person desiring to manufacture, sell, export, import, store, or purchase explosives or ingredients, or to keep explosives or ingredients in his possession, shall make application for a license, which application shall state, under oath, the name of the applicant; the place of birth; whether native born or naturalized citizen of the United States of America; if a naturalized citizen, the date and place of naturalization; business in which engaged; the amount and kind of explosives or ingredients which during the past six months have been purchased, disposed of, or used by him; the amount and kind of explosives or ingredients now on hand; whether sales, if any, have been made to jobbers, wholesalers, retailers, or consumers; the kind of license to be issued, and the kind and amount of explosives or ingredients to be authorized by the license; and such further information as the Director of the Bureau of Mines may, by rule, from time to time require.

Applications for vendor's, purchaser's, or foreman's licenses shall be made to such officers of the State, Territory, or dependency having jurisdiction in the district within which the explosives or ingredients are to be sold or used, and having power to administer oaths as may be designated by the Director of the Bureau of Mines, who shall issue the same in the name of such director. Such officers shall be entitled to receive from the applicant a fee of 25 cents for each license issued. They shall keep an accurate record of all licenses issued in manner and form to be prescribed by the Director of the Bureau of Mines, to whom they shall make reports from time to time as may be by rule issued by the director required. The necessary blanks and blank records shall be furnished to such officers by the said director. Licensing officers shall be subject to removal for cause by the Director of the Bureau of Mines, and all licenses issued by them shall be subject to revocation by the Director as provided in section eleven.

Sec. 13. That the President, by and with the advice and consent of the Senate, may appoint in each State and in Alaska an explosives inspector, whose duty it shall be, under the direction of the Director of the Bureau of Mines, to see that this Act is faithfully executed and observed. Each such inspector shall receive a salary of $2,400 per annum. He may at any time be detailed for service by said director in the District of Columbia or in any State, Territory, or dependency of the United States. All additional employees required in carrying out the provisions of this Act shall be appointed by the Director of the Bureau of

Mines, subject to the approval of the Secretary of the Interior.

Sec. 14. That it shall be unlawful for any person to represent himself as having a license issued under this Act, when he has not such a license, or as having a license different in form or in conditions from the one which he in fact has, or without proper authority make, cause to be made, issue or exhibit anything purporting or pretending to be such license, or intended to mislead any person into believing it is such a license, or to refuse to exhibit his license to any peace officer, Federal or State, or representative of the Bureau of Mines.

Sec. 15. That no inspector or other employee of the Bureau of Mines shall divulge any information obtained in the course of his duties under this Act regarding the business of any licensee, or applicant for license, without authority from the applicant for license or from the Director of the Bureau of Mines.

Sec. 16. That every person authorized under this Act to manufacture or store explosives or ingredients shall clearly mark and define the premises on which his plant or magazine may be and shall conspicuously display thereon the words "Explosives—Keep Off."

Sec. 17. That no person without the consent of the owner or his authorized agents, except peace officers, the Director of the Bureau of Mines and persons designated by him in writing, shall be in or upon any plant or premises on which explosives are manufactured or stored, or be in or upon any magazine premises on which explosives are stored; nor shall any person discharge any firearms or throw or place any explosives or inflammable bombs at, on, or against any such plant or magazine premises, or cause the same to be done.

Sec. 18. That the Director of the Bureau of Mines is hereby authorized to make rules and regulations for carrying into effect this Act, subject to the approval of the Secretary of the Interior.

Sec. 19. That any person violating any of the provisions of this Act, or any rules or regulations made thereunder, shall be guilty of a misdemeanor and shall be punished by a fine of not more than $5,000 or by imprisonment not more than one year, or by both such fine and imprisonment.

Sec. 20. That the Director of the Bureau of Mines is hereby authorized to investigate all explosions and fires which may occur in mines, quarries, factories, warehouses, magazines, houses, cars, boats, conveyances, and all places in which explosives or the ingredients thereof are manufactured, transported, stored, or used, and shall, in his discretion, report his findings, in such manner as he may deem fit, to the proper Federal or State authorities, to the end that if such explosion has been brought about by a willful act the person or persons causing such act may be proceeded against and brought to justice; or, if said explosion has been brought about by accidental means, that precautions may be taken to prevent similar accidents from occurring. In the prosecution of such investigations the employees of the Bureau of Mines are hereby granted the authority to enter the premises where such explosion or fire has occurred, to examine plans, books, and papers, to administer oaths to, and to examine all witnesses and persons concerned, without let or hindrance on the part of the owner, lessee, operator, or agent thereof.

Sec. 21. That the Director of the Bureau of Mines, with the approval of the President, is hereby authorized to utilize such agents, agencies, and all officers of the United States and of the several States, Territories, dependencies, and municipalities thereof, and the District of Columbia, in the execution of this Act, and all agents, agencies, and all officers of the United States and of the several States and Territories, dependencies, and municipalities thereof, and the District of Columbia, shall hereby have full authority for all acts done by them in the execution of this Act when acting by the direction of the Bureau of Mines.

Sec. 22. That for the enforcement of the provisions of this Act, including personal services in the District of Columbia and elsewhere, and including supplies, equipment, expenses of traveling and subsistence, and for the purchase and hire of animal-drawn or motor-propelled passenger-carrying vehicles, and upkeep of same, and for every other expense incident to the enforcement of the provisions of this Act, there is hereby appropriated, out of any money in the Treasury not otherwise appropriated, the sum of $300,000, or so much thereof as may be necessary: *Provided,* That not to exceed $10,000 shall be expended in the purchase of motor-propelled passenger-carrying vehicles. [Amended by act of July 1, 1918.]

1918—Act of March 28, 1918 (40 Stat. L., 490)—An Act Making appropriations to supply urgent deficiencies in appropriations for the fiscal year ending June 30, 1918, and prior fiscal years, on account of war expenses, and for other purposes.

* * * *

Bureau of Mines. War materials investigation: For inquiries and scientific and technologic investigations concerning the mining, preparation, treatment, and utilization of ores and other mineral substances which are particularly needed for carrying on the war, in connection with military and manufacturing purposes, and which have heretofore been largely imported, with a view to developing domestic sources of supply and substitutes for such ores and mineral products as are particularly needed, and conserving resources through the prevention of waste in the mining, quarrying, metallurgical, and other mineral industries; to inquire into the economic conditions affecting these industries; and including all equipment, supplies, expenses of travel, and subsistence, and not exceeding $5,340 for personal services in the District of Columbia; to continue available during the fiscal year nineteen hundred and nineteen, $150,000.

1918—Act of July 1, 1918 (40 Stat. L., 634, 671, 672)—An Act Making appropriations for sundry civil expenses of the Government for the fiscal year ending June thirtieth, nineteen hundred and nineteen, and for other purposes.

* * * *

That any license issued under the Act of October sixth, nineteen hundred and seventeen, may be canceled by the Director of the Bureau of Mines if the person to whom such license was issued shall, after notice and an opportunity to be heard, be found to have violated any of the provisions of the Act.

That platinum, iridium, and palladium and compounds thereof are hereby made subject to the terms, conditions, and limitations of said Act of October sixth, nineteen hundred and seventeen, and the Director of the Bureau of Mines is hereby authorized, under rules and regulations approved by the Secretary of the Interior, to limit the sale, possession, and the use of said material.

* * * *

For purchase or lease of necessary land, where and under such conditions as the Secretary of the Interior may direct, for the headquarters of mine-rescue cars and construction of neccessary railway sidings and housing for the same, or as the site of an experimental mine and a plant for studying explosives, $1,000: *Provided,* That the Secretary of the Interior is authorized to accept any suitable land or lands, buildings, or improvements, that may be donated for said purpose and to enter into leases for periods not exceeding ten years, subject to annual appropriations by Congress.

* * * *

The purchase of supplies and equipment or the procurement of services for the Bureau of Mines outside of the District of Columbia, hereafter may be made in open market in the manner common among business men when the aggregate amount of the purchase does not exceed $50;

Government Fuel Yard: The Secretary of the Interior is authorized and directed to establish in the District of Columbia storage and distributing yards for the storage of fuel for the use of and delivery to all branches of the Federal Service and the municipal government in the District of Columbia and such parts thereof as may be situated immediately without the District of Columbia and economically can be supplied therefrom, and to select, purchase, contract for, and distribute all fuel required by the said services. Authority is granted the Secretary of the Interior, in connection with the establishment of the said yards, to procure by purchase, requisition for immediate use, condemnation, or lease for such period as may be necessary, land, wharves, and railroad trestles and siding requisite therefor. All branches of the Federal service and the municipal government in the District of Columbia, from and after the establishment of the said fuel yards, shall purchase all fuel from the Secretary of the Interior and make payment therefor from applicable appropriations at the actual cost thereof to the United States, including all expenses connected therewith;

For the establishment of the fuel storage and distributing yards herein authorized, including the procurement of the necssary land, wharves, railroad sidings, and trestles; storing, handling, and distributing equipment, including motor-propelled passenger-carrying vehicles for inspectors; and all other expenses requisite for and incident thereto, including personal services in the District of Columbia; $432,300, to be available immediately.

* * * *

That no part of any moneys herein or hereafter appropriated shall be used for the purpose of taking over or in any way interfering with the yards or coal dumps or other facilities for storage and distribution of coal that have been used and occupied in the past year by coal dealers for supplying the general public.

1918—Act of October 5, 1918 (40 Stat. L., 1009)—An Act To provide further for the national security and defense by encouraging the production, conserving the supply, and controlling the distribution of those ores, metals, and minerals which have formerly been largely imported, or of which there is or may be an inadequate supply.

[Sec. 1]. That by reason of the existence of a state war, it is essential to the national security and defense, and to the successful prosecution of the war, and for the support and maintenance of the Army and Navy, to provide for an adequate and increased supply, to facilitate the production, and to provide for an equitable, economical, and better distribution of the following-named mineral substances and ores, minerals, intermediate metallurgical products, metals, alloys, and chemical compounds thereof, to wit: Antimony, arsenic, ball clay, bismuth, bromine, cerium, chalk, chromium, cobalt, corundum, emery, fluorspar, ferrosilicon, fuller's earth, graphite, grinding pebbles, iridium, kaolin, magnesite, manganese, mercury, mica, molybdenum, osmium, sodium, platinum, palladium, paper clay, phosphorus, potassium, pyrites, radium, sulphur, thorium, tin, titanium, tungsten, uranium, vanadium, and zirconium, as the President may from time to time, determine to be necessary for the purposes aforesaid, and as to which there is at the time of such determination, a present or prospective inadequacy of supply. The aforesaid substances mentioned in any such determination are hereinafter referred to as necessaries.

Sec. 2. That the President is authorized from time to time to purchase such necessaries and to enter into, to accept, to transfer, and to assign contracts for the production or purchase of same, to provide storage facilities for and store the same, to provide or improve transportation facilities, and to use, distribute, or allocate said necessaries, or to sell the same at reasonable prices, but such sales made during the war shall not be at a price less than the purchase or cost of production thereof: *Provided,* That no such contract of purchase shall cover a period longer than two years after the termination of the war.

The President is further authorized, upon finding that importation into the United States of any of the necessaries covered by this Act is likely to result in a loss to the United Sates on any necessaries which it may have acquired hereunder, to ascertain, fix, and proclaim such rate of duty upon such imported necessaries as shall be sufficient to adequately protect the United States from any such loss.

The funds provided by section six hereof shall be used in carrying out the powers granted by this section, and all moneys received by the United States from or in connection with the disposal of such necessaries, shall be used as a revolving fund for further carrying out the purposes of this Act. Any balance of such moneys remaining when the object of this Act has been accomplished, shall, as collected, received, and on hand and available, be covered into the Treasury as miscellaneous receipts.

Sec. 3. That the President is authorized to requisition and take over any of said necessaries and to use, distribute, allocate, or sell the same; and also to requisition and take over any undeveloped mine, and any idle or partially operated smelter, or plant, or part thereof, producing or, in his judgment capable of producing said necessaries, or either of them, and to develop and operate such mine or deposit or such smelter or plant, either through the agencies hereinafter mentioned, or under lease or royalty agreement, or in any other manner, and to store, use, distribute, allocate, or sell the products thereof: *Provided,* That no ores or metals, the principal money value of which consists in metals or minerals other than those specifically enumerated in section one hereof, shall be subject to requisition under the provisions of this Act. Whenever the President shall determine that the further use or operation by the Government of any such land, deposit, mine, smelter, or plant, or part thereof, so acquired, is no longer essential for the objects aforesaid, the same shall be returned to the person, firm or corporation entitled thereto. The United States shall make just compensation, determined by the President, for the taking over, use, occupation, or operation by the Government of any such necessaries, or any such land, deposit, mine, smelter, or plant, or part thereof. If the compensation so determined be unsatisfactory to the person, firm, or corporation entitled thereto, such person, firm, or corporation shall be paid seventy-five per centum of the amount so determined and shall be entitled to sue the United States to recover such further sum as added to said seventy-five per centum will make up such amount as will be just compensation, in the manner provided by section twenty-four, paragraph twenty, and section one hundred and forty-five, of the Judicial Code.

The President is authorized to require statements and reports, to examine books and papers, and to prescribe such rules and regulations as he may deem appropriate for carrying out the purposes of this Act. The fund provided by section six hereof may be used in carrying out the purposes of this Act, and all moneys received by the United States from or in connection with the use, operation, or disposal of any such necessaries, land, deposit, mine, smelter, or plant, or part thereof, shall be used as a revolving fund for further carrying out the purposes of this Act. Any balance of such moneys remaining when the objects of this Act have been accomplished, shall, as collected, received, and on hand and available, be covered into the Treasury as miscellaneous receipts.

Sec. 4. That any person who shall neglect or refuse to comply with any order or requisition made by the President pursuant to the provisions of this Act, or who shall obstruct or attempt to obstruct the enforcement of or the compliance with any such requisition or order, or who shall violate any of the provisions of this Act, or any rule or regulation adopted hereunder, shall, upon conviction, be fined not exceeding $5,000, or be imprisoned for not more than two years, or both.

Sec. 5. That the sum of $500,000 is hereby appropriated, out of any moneys in the Treasury not otherwise appropriated, to be available until June thirtieth, nineteen hundred and nineteen, for the payment of all administrative expenses under this Act, including personal services, travelling and subsistence expenses, the payment of rent, the purchase of equipment, supplies, postage, printing, publications, and such other articles, both in the District of Columbia and elsewhere, as the President may deem essential and proper.

Sec. 6. That the sum of $50,000,000 is hereby appropriated, out of any moneys in the Treasury not otherwise appropriated, which, together with all moneys received from time to time under the provisions of this Act, all of which shall be credited to said appropriation, shall be used as a revolving fund for carrying out the objects of this Act, and for the purpose of making all payments and disbursements, including just compensation under section three, by this Act authorized: *Provided,* That no part of this appropriation shall be expended for the purposes described in the last preceding section: *Provided further,* That a detailed report of all operations under this Act, including all receipts and disbursements, shall be filed with the Secretary of the Senate and Clerk of the House of Representatives on or before the twenty-fifth day of each month, covering the preceding month's operation. Any balance of said revolving fund remaining when the objects of this Act have been accomplished, shall, as collected, received, and on hand and available, be covered into the Treasury as miscellaneous receipts.

Sec. 7. That the President is authorized to exercise each, every, or any power and authority hereby vested in him, and to expend the moneys herein appropriated or provided for, or any part or parts thereof, by and through such officer or officers, department or departments, board or boards, agent, agents, or agencies as he shall create or designate, from time to time, for the purpose. He may fix the reasonable compensation for the performances of such services, but no official or employee of the United States shall receive any additional compensation for such services except as now permitted by law: *Provided,* That no person employed under the provisions of this Act shall be paid any salary or compensation in excess of that paid for similar or like services rendered in executive departments of the Government.

Sec. 8. No person having a pecuniary interest in any transaction in pursuance of this Act shall have any official connection under this Act with such transaction. Any person violating this provision shall forfeit to the Government all proceeds which he shall have received from such transaction, and upon due conviction of such violation shall be fined not exceeding $10,000 or imprisonment not exceeding ten years.

Sec. 9. That the President is authorized, if in his judgment such action be necessary or useful for the objects of this Act, to form one or more corporations under the laws of any State, Territory, District, or possession of the United States, for the purpose of carrying out the powers or any of the powers hereby authorized. The capital stock of any such corporation shall be such as the President may determine, but the total capital stock for all corporations so formed shall not exceed in the aggregate the appropriation of $50,000,000, made by section six hereof. Said appropriation, or any part thereof, may be used by the President in subscribing on behalf of the United States, through such person or persons as he may designate, to the capital stock of such corporation or corporations, and the capital and assets of any such corporation or corporations, together with all additions thereto under sections two and three hereof, may be used in carrying out the objects of this Act. The directorate and organization of such corporation or corporations shall be such as the President may prescribe, and such corporation or corporations shall have all such charter powers as may be deemed necessary or desirable by the President to enable it or them to accomplish the objects of this Act. The capital stock of any such corporation or corporations shall be held and voted for the exclusive benefit of the United States, through such person or persons as the President may designate.

Sec. 10. Upon the proclamation of peace[1] the President shall proceed as rapidly as possible to wind up and terminate all transactions under this Act, and to dispose as fast as practicable of all property acquired thereunder, and after said proclamation of peace no contracts shall be made, property acquired, or other transaction performed under this Act except such as shall be necessary for the purpose of this section and incidental thereto, and two years after such proclamation of peace this Act shall cease to have effect and all powers conferred thereby shall end: *Provided,* That the termination of this Act shall not prevent the subsequent collection of any moneys due the United States, nor shall it affect any act done or any right or obligation accrued or accruing, or any suit or proceeding had or commenced before such termination, but all such collections, rights, obligations, suits, and proceedings shall continue as if this Act had not terminated, and any offense committed or liability incurred prior thereto shall be prosecuted in the same manner and with the same punishment and effect as if this Act had not terminated.

Sec. 11. That employment under the provisions of this Act shall not exempt any person from military service under the provisions of the selective draft law approved May eighteenth, nineteen hundred and seventeen, or any Act amendatory thereto.

[1] July 2, 1921.

Sec. 12. That if any section or provision of this Act shall be declared invalid for any reason whatsoever, such invalidity shall not be construed to affect the validity of any other section or provision hereof.[1]

1919—Act of February 25, 1919 (40 Stat. L., 1154)—An Act Authorizing the Secretary of the Interior to make investigations, through the Bureau of Mines, of lignite coals and peat, to determine the practicability of their utilization as a fuel and in producing commercial products.

[Sec. 1]. That the Secretary of the Interior is hereby authorized and directed to make experiments and investigations, through the Bureau of Mines, of lignite coals and peat, to determine the commercial and economic practicability of their utilization in producing fuel oil, gasoline substitutes, ammonia, tar solid fuels, gas for power and other purposes; and there is hereby appropriated, out of the funds in the Treasury not otherwise appropriated, the sum of $100,000, or so much thereof as may be needed, to conduct such experiments and investigations, including personal services in the District of Columbia and elsewhere, and including supplies, equipment, expenses of traveling and subsistence, and for every other expense incident to this work.

Sec. 2. The Secretary of the Interior is authorized and directed to sell or otherwise dispose of any property, plant, or machinery purchased or acquired under the provisions of this Act, as soon as the experiments and investigations hereby authorized have been concluded, and report the results of such experiments and investigations to Congress.

1919—Act of March 2, 1919 (40 Stat. L., 1272)—An Act To provide relief in cases of contracts connected with the prosecution of the war, and for other purposes.

* * * *

Sec. 5. That the Secretary of the Interior be, and he hereby is, authorized to adjust, liquidate, and pay such net losses as have been suffered by any person, firm, or corporation, by reason of producing or preparing to produce, either manganese, chrome, pyrites,

[1] "By executive order of November 11, 1918, the administration of the act was delegated to the Secretary of the Interior. On that date the armistice ended hostilities. As the act primarily provided for insuring production for war purposes, it was not a reconstruction measure and further legislation was required for that purpose."—Bureau of Mines, Annual Report, 1919, p. 64.

or tungsten in compliance with the request or demand of the Department of the Interior, the War Industries Board, the War Trade Board, the Shipping Board, or the Emergency Fleet Corporation to supply the urgent needs of the Nation in the prosecution of the war; said minerals being enumerated in the Act of Congress approved October fifth, nineteen hundred and eighteen, entitled "An Art to provide further for the national security and defense by encouraging the production, conserving the supply, and controlling the distribution of those ores, metals, and minerals which have formerly been largely imported, or of which there is or may be an inadequate supply."

The said Secretary shall make such adjustments and payments in each case as he shall determine to be just and equitable; that the decision of said Secretary shall be conclusive and final, subject to the limitation hereinafter provided; that all payments and expenses incurred by said Secretary, including personal services, traveling and subsistence expenses, supplies, postage, printing, and all other expenses incident to the proper prosecution of this work, both in the District of Columbia and elsewhere, as the Secretary of the Interior may deem essential and proper, shall be paid from the funds appropriated by the said Act of October fifth, nineteen hundred and eighteen, and that said funds and appropriations shall continue to be available for said purpose until such time as the said Secretary shall have fully exercised the authority herein granted and performed and completed the duties hereby provided and imposed: *Provided, however,* That the payments and disbursements made under the provisions of this section for and in connection with the payments and settlements of the claims herein described, and the said expenses of administration shall in no event exceed the sum of $8,500,000: *And provided further,* That said Secretary shall consider, approve, and dispose of only such claims as shall be made hereunder and filed with the Department of the Interior within three monhts from and after the approval of this Act: *And provided further,* That no claim shall be allowed or paid by said Secretary unless it shall appear to the satisfaction of the said Secretary that the expenditures so made or obligations so incurred by the claimant were made in good faith for or upon property which contained either manganese, chrome, pyrites, or tungsten in sufficient quantities to be of commercial importance: *And provided further,* That no claims shall be paid unless it shall appear to the satisfaction of said Secretary that moneys were invested or obligations were incurred subsequent to April sixth, nineteen hundred and seventeen, and prior to November twelfth, nineteen hundred and eighteen, in a legitimate attempt to produce either manganese, chrome, pyrites, or tungsten for the needs of the Nation for the prosecution of the war, and that no profits of any kind shall be included in the allowance of any of said claims, and that no investment for merely speculative purposes shall be recognized in any manner by said Secretary: *And provided further,* That the settlement of any claim arising under the provisions of this section shall not bar the United States Government, through any of its duly authorized agencies, or any committee of Congress hereafter duly appointed, from the right of review of such settlement, nor the right to recover any money paid by the Government to any party under and by virtue of the provisions of this section, if the Government has been defrauded, and the right of recovery in all such cases shall extend to the executors, administrators, heirs, and assigns of any party.

That a report of all operations under this section, including receipts and disbursements, shall be made to Congress on or before the first Monday in December of each year.

That nothing in this section shall be construed to confer jurisdiction upon any court to entertain a suit against the United States: *Provided further,* That in determining the net losses of any claimant the Secretary of the Interior shall, among other things, take into consideration and charge to the claimant, the then market value of any ores or minerals on hand belonging to the claimant, and also the salvage or usable value of any machinery or other appliances which may be claimed was purchased to equip said mine for the purpose of complying with the request or demand of the agencies of the Government above mentioned in the manner aforesaid.[1]

1919—Act of July 19, 1919 (41 Stat. L., 163, 199)—An Act Making appropriations for sundry civil expenses of the Government for the fiscal year ending June 30, 1920, and for other purposes.

* * * *

For the purchase or lease of necessary land, where and under such conditions as the Secretary of the Interior may direct, for headquarters of mine-rescue cars and construction of necessary railway sidings and housing for the same, or as the site of an experimental mine and a plant for studying explosives, $1,000: *Provided,* That the Secretary of the Interior is authorized to accept any suitable land or lands, buildings, or improvements, that may be donated for said purpose and to enter into leases for periods not exceeding ten years, subject to annual appropriation by Congress.

1920—Act of February 25, 1920 (41 Stat. L., 437)—An Act To promote the mining of coal, phosphate, oil, oil shale, gas, and sodium on the public domain.

[Sec. 1]. That deposits of coal, phosphate, sodium, oil, oil shale, or gas, and lands containing such deposits owned by the United

---

[1] "For the execution of this provision a commission of three members, known as the War Minerals Relief Commission, was appointed by the Secretary of the Interior for the purpose of reviewing the claims and making recommendations to the Secretary, in whom final action is vested. * * * The Director of the Bureau of Mines is authorized to conduct examination of properties, accounting investigations, office routine, and the administrative work of the Commission."—Bureau of Mines, Annual Report, 1920, p. 31.

LAWS

States, including those in national forests, but excluding lands acquired under the Act known as the Appalachian Forest Act, approved March 1, 1911 (Thirty-sixth Statutes, page 961), and those in national parks, and in lands withdrawn or reserved for military or naval uses or purposes, except as hereinafter provided, shall be subject to disposition in the form and manner provided by this Act to citizens of the United States, or to any association of such persons, or to any corporation organized under the laws of the United States, or of any State or Territory thereof, and in the case of coal, oil, oil shale, or gas, to municipalities: *Provided,* That the United States reserves the right to extract helium from all gas produced from lands permitted, leased, or otherwise granted under the provisions of this Act, under such rules and regulations as shall be prescribed by the Secretary of the Interior: *Provided further,* That in the extraction of helium from gas produced from such lands, it shall be so extracted as to cause no substantial delay in the delivery of gas produced from the well to the purchaser thereof: *And provided further,* That citizens of another country, the laws, customs, or regulations of which, deny similar or like privileges to citizens or corporations of this country, shall not by stock ownership, stock holding, or stock control, own any interest in any lease acquired under the provisions of this Act.

COAL

Sec. 2. That the Secretary of the Interior is authorized to, and upon the petition of any qualified applicant shall, divide any of the coal lands or the deposits of coal, classified and unclassified, owned by the United States, outside of the Territory of Alaska, into leasing tracts of forty acres each, or multiples thereof, and in such form as, in the opinion of the Secretary of the Interior, will permit the most economical mining of the coal in such tracts, but in no case exceeding two thousand five hundred and sixty acres in any one leasing tract, and thereafter the Secretary of the Interior shall, in his discretion, and upon the request of any qualified applicant or on his own motion, from time to time, offer such lands or deposits of coal for leasing, and shall award leases thereon by competitive bidding or by such other methods as he may by general regulations adopt, to any qualified applicant: *Provided,* That the Secretary is hereby authorized, in awarding leases for coal lands heretofore improved and occupied or claimed in good faith, to consider and recognize equitable rights of such occupants or claimants: *Provided further,* That where prospecting or exploratory work is necessary to determine the existence or workability of coal deposits in any unclaimed, undeveloped area, the Secretary of the Interior may issue, to applicants qualified under this Act, prospecting permits for a term of two years, for not exceeding two thousand five hundred and sixty acres; and if within said period of two years thereafter, and permittee shows to the Secretary that the land contains coal in commercial quantities, the permittee shall be entitled to a lease under this Act for all or part of the land in his permit: *And provided further,* That no lease of coal under this Act shall be approved or issued until after notice of the proposed lease, or offering for lease, has been given for thirty days in a newspaper of general circulation in the county in which the lands or deposits are situated: *And provided further,* That no company or corporation operating a common carrier railroad shall be given or hold a permit or lease under the provisions of this Act for any coal deposits except for its own use for railroad purposes; and such limitations of use shall be expressed in all permits and leases issued to such companies or corporations, and no such company or corporation shall receive or hold more than one permit or lease for each two hundred miles of its railroad line within the State in which said property is situated, exclusive of spurs of switches and exclusive of branch lines built to connect the leased coal with the railroad, and also exclusive of parts of the railroad operated mainly by power produced otherwise than by steam: *And provided further,* That nothing herein shall preclude such a railroad of less than two hundred miles in length from securing and holding one permit or lease hereunder.

Sec. 3. That any person, association, or corporation holding a lease of coal lands or coal deposits under this Act may, with the approval of the Secretary of the Interior, upon a finding by him that it will be for the advantage of the lessee and the United States, secure modifications of his or its original lease by including additional coal lands or coal deposits contiguous to those embraced in such lease, but in no event shall the total area embraced in such modified lease exceed in the aggregate two thousand five hundred and sixty acres.

Sec. 4. That upon satisfactory showing by any lessee to the Secretary of the Interior that all of the workable deposits of coal within a tract covered by his or its lease will be exhausted, worked out, or removed within three years thereafter, the Secretary of the Interior may, within his discretion, lease to such lessee an additional tract of land or coal deposits, which including the coal area remaining in the existing lease, shall not exceed two thousand five hundred and sixty acres, through the same procedure and under the same conditions as in the case of an original lease.

Sec. 5. That if, in the judgment of the Secretary of the Interior, the public interest will be subserved thereby, lessees holding under lease areas not exceeding the maximum permitted under this Act may consolidate their leases through the surrender of the original leases and the inclusion of such areas in a new lease of not to exceed two thousand five hundred and sixty acres of contiguous lands.

Sec. 6. That where coal or phosphate lands aggregating two thousand five hundred and sixty acres and subject to lease hereunder do not exist as contiguous areas, the Secretary of the Interior is authorized, if, in his opinion the interest of the public and of the lessee will be thereby subserved, to embrace in a single lease noncontiguous tracts which can be operated as a single mine or unit.

Sec. 7. That for the privilege of mining or extracting the coal in the lands covered by the lease the lessee shall pay to the United States such royalties as may be specified in the lease, which shall be fixed in advance of offering the same, and which shall not be less than 5 cents per ton of two thousand pounds, due and payable at the end of each third month succeeding that of the extraction of the coal from the mine, and an annual rental, payable at the date of such lease and annually thereafter, on the lands or coal deposits covered by such lease, at such rate as may be fixed by the Secretary of the Interior prior to offering the same, which shall not be less than 25 cents per acre for the first year thereafter, not less than 50 cents per acre for the second, third, fourth, and fifth years, respectively, and not less than $1 per acre for each and every year thereafter during the continuance of the lease, except that such rental for any year shall be credited against the royalties as they accrue for that year. Leases shall be for indeterminate periods upon condition of diligent development and continued operation of the mine or mines, except when such operation shall be interrupted by strikes, the elements, or casualties not attributable to the lessee, and upon the further condition that at the end of each twenty-year period succeeding the date of the lease such readjustment of terms and conditions may be made as the Secretary of the Interior may determine, unless otherwise provided by law at the time of the expiration of such periods: *Provided,* That the Secretary of the Interior may, if in his judgment the public interest will be subserved thereby, in lieu of the provision herein contained requiring continuous operation of the mine or mines, provide in the lease for the payment of an annual advance royalty upon a minimum number of tons of coal, which in no case shall aggregate less than the amount of rentals herein provided for: *Provided further,* That the Secretary of the Interior may permit suspension of operation under such lease for not to exceed six months at any one time when market conditions are such that the lease can not be operated except at a loss.

Sec. 8. That in order to provide for the supply of strictly local domestic needs for fuel, the Secretary of the Interior may, under such rules and regulations as he may prescribe in advance, issue limited licenses or permits to individuals or associations of individuals to prospect for, mine, and take for their use but not for sale, coal from the public lands without payment of royalty for the coal mined or the land occupied, on such conditions not inconsistent with this Act as in his opinion will safeguard the public interests: *Provided,* That this privilege shall not extend to any corporations: *Provided further,* That in the case of municipal corporations the Secretary of the Interior may issue such limited license or permit, for not to exceed three hundred and twenty acres for a municipality of not less than one hundred thousand population, and not to exceed one thousand two hundred and eighty acres for a municipality of not less than one hundred thousand and not more than one hundred and fifty thousand population and not to exceed two thousand five hundred and sixty acres for a municipality of one hundred and fifty thousand population or more, the land to be selected within the State wherein the municipal applicant may be located, upon condition that such municipal corporations will mine the coal therein under proper conditions and dispose of the same without profit to residents of such municipality for household use:

And provided further, That the acquisition or holding of a lease under the preceding sections of this Act shall be no bar to the holding of such tract or operation of such mine under said limited license.

PHOSPHATES

Sec. 9. That the Secretary of the Interior is hereby authorized to lease to any applicant qualified under this Act any lands belonging to the United States containing deposits of phosphates, under such restrictions and upon such terms as are herein specified, through advertisement, competitive bidding, or such other methods as the Secretary of the Interior may by general regulation adopt.

Sec. 10. That each lease shall be for not to exceed two thousand five hundred and sixty acres of land to be described by the legal subdivisions of the public land surveys, if surveyed; if unsurveyed, to be surveyed by the Government at the expense of the applicant for lease, in accordance with rules and regulations prescribed by the Secretary of the Interior with the lands leased shall be conformed to and taken in accordance with the legal subdivisions of such survey; deposits made to cover expense of surveys shall be deemed appropriated for that purpose; and any excess deposits shall be repaid to the person, association, or corporation making such deposits or their legal representatives: *Provided,* That the land embraced in any one lease shall be in compact form, the length of which shall not exceed two and one half times its width.

Sec. 11. That for the privilege of mining or extracting the phosphates or phosphate rock covered by the lease the lessee shall pay to the United States such royalties as may be specified in the lease, which shall be fixed by the Secretary of the Interior in advance of offering the same, which shall not be less than 2 per centum of the gross value of the output of phosphates or phosphate rock at the mine, due and payable at the end of each third month succeeding that of the sale or other disposition of the phosphates or phosphate rock, and an annual rental payable at the date of such lease and annually thereafter on the area covered by such lease at such rate as may be fixed by the Secretary of the Interior prior to offering the lease, which shall be not less than 25 cents per acre for the first year thereafter, 50 cents per acre for the second, third, fourth, and fifth years, respectively, and $1 per acre for each and every year thereafter during the continuance of the lease, except that such rental for any year shall be credited against the royalties as they accrue for that year. Leases shall be for indeterminate periods upon condition of a minimum annual production, except when operation shall be interrupted by strikes, the elements, or casualties not attributable to the lessee, and upon the further condition that at the end of each twenty-year period succeeding the date of the lease such readjustment of terms and conditions shall be made as the Secretary of the Interior shall determine unless otherwise provided by law at the time of the expiration of such periods: *Provided,* That the Secretary of the Interior may permit suspension of operation under such lease for not exceeding twelve months at any one time when market conditions are such that the lease can not be operated except at a loss.

Sec. 12. That any qualified applicant to whom the Secretary of the Interior may grant a lease to develop and extract phosphates, or phosphate rock, under the provisions of this Act shall have the right to use so much of the surface of unappropriated and unentered lands, not exceeding forty acres, as may be determined by the Secretary of the Interior to be necessary for the proper prospecting for or development, extraction, treatment, and removal of such mineral deposits.

OIL AND GAS

Sec. 13. That the Secretary of the Interior is hereby authorized, under such necessary and proper rules and regulations as he may prescribe, to grant to any applicant qualified under this Act a prospecting permit, which shall give the exclusive right, for a period not exceeding two years, to prospect for oil or gas upon not to exceed two thousand five hundred and sixty acres of land wherein such deposits belong to the United States and are not within any known geological structure of a producing oil or gas field upon condition that the permittee shall begin drilling operations within six months from the date of the permit, and shall, within one year from and after the date of permit, drill one or more wells for oil or gas to a depth of not less than five hundred feet each, unless valuable deposits of oil or gas shall be sooner discovered, and shall, within two years from date of the permit, drill for oil or gas to an aggregate depth of not less than two thousand feet unless valuable deposits of oil or gas shall be sooner discovered. The Secretary of the Interior may, if he shall find that the permittee has been unable with the exercise of diligence to test the land in the time granted by the permit, extend any such permit for such time, not exceeding two years, and upon such conditions as he shall prescribe. Whether the lands sought in any such application and permit are surveyed or unsurveyed the applicant shall, prior to filing his application for permit, locate such lands in a reasonably compact form and according to the legal subdivisions of the public land surveys if the land be surveyed; and in an approximately square or rectangular tract if the land be an unsurveyed tract, the length of which shall not exceed two and one-half times its width, and if he shall cause to be erected upon the land for which a permit is sought a monument not less than four feet high, at some conspicuous place thereon, and shall post a notice in writing on or near said monument, stating that an application for permit will be made within thirty days after date of posting said notice, the name of the applicant, the date of the notice, and such a general description of the land to be covered by such permit by reference to courses and distances from such monument and such other natural objects and permanent monuments as will reasonably identify the land, stating the amount thereof in acres, he shall during the period of thirty days following such marking and posting, be entitled to preference right over others to a permit for the land so identified. The applicant shall, within ninety days after receiving a permit mark each of the corners of the tract described in the permit upon the ground with substantial monuments, so that the boundaries can be readily traced on the ground, and shall post in a conspicuous place upon the lands a notice that such permit has been granted and description of the lands covered thereby: *Provided,* That in the Territory of Alaska prospecting permits not more than five in number may be granted to any qualified applicant for periods not exceeding four years, actual drilling operations shall begin within two years from date of permit, and oil and gas wells shall be drilled to a depth of not less than five hundred feet, unless valuable deposits of oil or gas shall be sooner discovered, within three years from date of the permit and to an aggregate depth of not less than two thousand feet unless valuable deposits of oil or gas shall be sooner discovered, within four years from date of permit: *Provided further,* That in said Territory the applicant shall have a preference right over others to a permit for land identified by temporary monuments and notice posted on or near the same for six months following such marking and posting, and upon receiving a permit he shall mark the corners of the tract described in the permit upon the ground with substantial monuments within one year after receiving such permit.

Sec. 14. That upon establishing to the satisfaction of the Secretary of the Interior that valuable deposits of oil or gas have been discovered within the limits of the land embraced in any permit, the permittee shall be entitled to a lease for one-fourth of the land embraced in the prospecting permit: *Provided,* That the permittee shall be granted a lease for as much as one hundred and sixty acres of said lands, if there be that number of acres within the permit. The area to be selected by the permittee, shall be in compact form and, if surveyed, to be described by the legal subdivisions of the public-land surveys; if unsurveyed, to be surveyed by the Government at the expense of the applicant for lease in accordance with rules and regulations to be prescribed by the Secretary of the Interior and the lands leased shall be conformed to and taken in accordance with the legal subdivisions of such surveys; deposits made to cover expense of surveys shall be deemed appropriated for that purpose, and any excess deposits may be repaid to the person or persons making such deposit or their legal representatives. Such leases shall be for a term of twenty years upon a royalty of 5 per centum in amount or value of the production and the annual payment in advance of a rental of $1 per acre, the rental paid for any one year to be credited against the royalties as they accrue for that year, with the right of renewal as prescribed in section 17 hereof. The permittee shall also be entitled to a preference right to a lease for the remainder of the land in his prospecting permit at a royalty of not less than $12\frac{1}{2}$ per centum in amount or value of the production, and under such other conditions as are fixed for oil or gas leases in this Act, the royalty to be determined by competitive bidding or fixed by such other method as the Secretary may by regulations prescribe: *Provided,* That the Secretary shall have the right to reject any or all bids.

Sec. 15. That until the permittee shall apply for lease to the one quarter of the permit area heretofore provided for he shall pay to the United States 20 per centum of the gross value of all oil or gas secured by him from the lands embraced within his permit and sold or otherwise disposed of or held by him for sale or other disposition.

Sec. 16. That all permits and leases of lands containing oil or gas, made or issued under the provisions of this Act, shall be subject to the condition that no wells shall be drilled within two hundred feet of any of the outer boundaries of the lands so permitted or leased, unless the adjoining lands have been patented or the title thereto otherwise vested in private owners, and to the further conditions that the permittee or lessee will, in conducting his explorations and mining operations, use all reasonable precautions to prevent waste of oil or gas developed in the land, or the entrance of water through wells drilled by him to the oil sands or oil-bearing strata, to the destruction or injury of the oil deposits. Violations of the provisions of this section shall constitute grounds for the forfeiture of the permit or lease, to be enforced through appropriate proceedings in courts of competent jurisdiction.

Sec. 17. That all unappropriated deposits of oil or gas situated within the known geologic structure of a producing oil or gas field and the unentered lands containing the same, not subject to preferential lease, may be leased by the Secretary of the Interior to the highest responsible bidder by competitive bidding under general regulations to qualified applicants in areas not exceeding six hundred and forty acres and in tracts which shall not exceed in length two and one-half times their width, such leases to be conditioned upon the payment by the lessee of such bonus as may be accepted and of such royalty as may be fixed in the lease. which shall not be less than $12\frac{1}{2}$ per centum in amount or value of the production, and the payment in advance of a rental of not less than $1 per acre per annum thereafter during the continuance of the lease, the rental paid for any one year to be credited against the royalties as they accrue for that year. Leases shall be for a period of twenty years, with the preferential right in the lessee to renew the same for successive periods of ten years upon such reasonable terms and conditions as may be prescribed by the Secretary of the Interior, unless otherwise provided by law at the time of the expiration of such periods. Whenever the average daily production of any oil well shall not exceed ten barrels per day, the Secretary of the Interior is authorized to reduce the royalty on future production when in his judgment the wells can not be successfully operated upon the royalty fixed in the lease. The provisions of this paragraph shall apply to all oil and gas leases made under this Act.

Sec. 18. That upon relinquishment to the United States, filed in the General Land Office within six months after approval of this Act, of all right, title, and interest claimed and possessed prior to July 3, 1910, and continuously since by the claimant or his predecessor in interest under the preëxisting placer mining law to any oil or gas bearing land upon which there has been drilled one or more oil or gas wells to discovery embraced in the Executive order of withdrawal issued September 27, 1909, and not within any naval petroleum reserve, and upon payment as royalty to the United States of an amount equal to the value at the time of production of one-eighth of all the oil or gas already produced except oil or gas used for production purposes on the claim, or unavoidably lost, from such land, the claimant, or his successor, if in possession of such land, undisputed by any other claimant prior to July 1, 1919, shall be entitled to a lease thereon from the United States for a period of twenty years, at a royalty of not less than 12½ per centum of all the oil or gas produced except oil or gas used for production purposes on the claim, or unavoidably lost: *Provided,* That not more than one-half of the area, but in no case to exceed three thousand two hundred acres, within the geologic oil or gas structure of a producing oil or gas field shall be leased to any one claimant under the provision of this section when the area of such geologic oil structure exceeds six hundred and forty acres. Any claimant or his successor, subject to this limitation, shall, however, have the right to select and receive the lease as in this section provided for that portion of his claim or claims equal to, but not in excess of, said one-half of the area of such geologic oil structure, but not more than three thousand two hundred acres.

All such leases shall be made and the amount of royalty to be paid for oil and gas produced, except oil or gas used for production purposes on the claim, or unavoidably lost, after the execution of such lease shall be fixed by the Secretary of the Interior under appropriate rules and regulations: *Provided, however,* That as to all like claims situated within any naval petroleum reserve the producing wells thereon only shall be leased, together with an area of land sufficient for the operation thereof, upon the terms and payment of royalties for past and future production as herein provided for in the leasing of claims. No wells shall be drilled in the land subject to this provision within six hundred and sixty feet of any such leased well without the consent of the lessee: *Provided, however,* That the President may, in his discretion, lease the remainder or any part of any such claim upon which such wells have been drilled, and in the event of such leasing said claimant or his successor shall have a preference right to such lease: *And provided further,* That he may permit the drilling of additional wells by the claimant or his successor within the limited area of six hundred and sixty feet theretofore provided for upon such terms and conditions as he may prescribe.

No claimant for a lease who has been guilty of any fraud or who had knowledge or reasonable grounds to know of any fraud, or who has not acted honestly and in good faith, shall be entitled to any of the benefits of this section.

Upon the delivery and acceptance of the lease, as in this section provided, all suits brought by the Government affecting such lands may be settled and adjusted in accordance herewith and all moneys impounded in such suits or under the Act entitled "An Act to amend an Act entitled 'An Act to protect the locators in good faith of oil and gas lands who shall have effected an actual discovery of oil or gas on the public lands of the United States, or their successors in interest,' approved March 2, 1911," approved August 25, 1914

(Thirty-eighth Statutes at Large, page 708), shall be paid over to the parties entitled thereto. In case of conflicting claimants for leases under this section, the Secretary of the Interior is authorized to grant leases to one or more of them as shall be deemed just. All leases hereunder shall inure to the benefit of the claimant and all persons claiming through or under him by lease, contract, or otherwise, as their interests may appear, subject, however, to the same limitation as to area and acreage as is provided for claimant in this section: *Provided,* That no claimant acquiring any interest in such lands since September 1, 1919, from a claimant on or since said date claiming or holding more than the maximum allowed claimant under this section shall secure a lease thereon or any interest therein, but the inhibition of this proviso shall not apply to an exchange of any interest in such lands made prior to the 1st day of January, 1920, which did not increase or reduce the area or acreage held or claimed in excess of said maximum by either party to the exchange: *Provided further,* That no lease or leases under this section shall be granted, nor shall any interest therein, inure to any person, association, or corporation for a greater aggregate area or acreage than the maximum in this section provided for.

Sec. 18a. That whenever the validity of any gas or petroleum placer claim under preëxisting law to land embraced in the Executive order of withdrawal issued September 27, 1909, has been or may hereafter be drawn in question on behalf of the United States in any departmental or judicial proceedings, the President is hereby authorized at any time within twelve months after the approval of this Act to direct the compromise and settlement of any such controversy upon such terms and conditions as may be agreed upon, to be carried out by an exchange or division of land or division of the proceeds of operation.

Sec. 19. That any person who on October 1, 1919, was a bona fide occupant or claimant of oil or gas lands under a claim initiated while such lands were not withdrawn from oil or gas location and entry, and who had previously performed all acts under then existing laws necessary to valid locations thereof except to make discovery, and upon which discovery had not been made prior to the passage of this Act, and who has performed work or expended on or for the benefit of such locations an amount equal in the aggregate of $250 for each location if application therefor shall be made within six months from the passage of this Act shall be entitled to prospecting permits thereon upon the same terms and conditions, and limitations as to acreage, as other permits provided for in this Act, or where any such person has heretofore made such discovery, he shall be entitled to a lease thereon under such terms as the Secretary of the Interior may prescribe unless otherwise provided for in section 18 hereof: *Provided,* That where such prospecting permit is granted upon land within any known geologic structure of a producing oil or gas field, the royalty to be fixed in any lease thereafter granted thereon or any portion thereof shall be not less than $12\frac{1}{2}$ per centum of all the oil or gas produced except oil or gas used for production purposes on the claim, or unavoidably lost: *Provided, however,* That the provisions of this section shall not apply to lands reserved for the use of the Navy: *Provided, however,* That no claimant for a permit or lease who has been guilty of any fraud or who had knowledge or reasonable grounds to know of any fraud, or who has not acted honestly and in good faith, shall be entitled to any of the benefits of this section.

All permits or leases hereunder shall inure to the benefit of the claimant and all persons claiming through or under him by lease, contract, or otherwise, as their interests may appear.

Sec. 20. In the case of lands bona fide entered as agricultural, and not withdrawn or classified as mineral at the time of entry, but not including lands claimed under any railroad grant, the entryman or patentee, or assigns, where assignment was made prior to January 1, 1918, if the entry has been patented with the mineral right reserved, shall be entitled to a preference right to a permit and to a lease, as herein provided, in case of discovery; and within an area not greater than a township such entryman and patentees, or assigns holding restricted patents may combine their holdings, not to exceed two thousand five hundred and sixty acres for the purpose of making joint application. Leases executed under this section and embracing only lands so entered shall provide for the payment of a royalty of not less than 12½ per centum as to such areas within the permit as may not be included within the discovery lease to which the permittee is entitled under section 14 thereof.

OIL SHALE

Sec. 21. That the Secretary of the Interior is hereby authorized to lease to any person or corporation qualified under this Act any deposits of oil shale belonging to the United States and the surface of so much of the public lands containing such deposits, or land adjacent thereto, as may be required for the extraction and reduction of the leased minerals, under such rules and regulations, not inconsistent with this Act, as he may prescribe; that no lease hereunder shall exceed five thousand one hundred and twenty acres of land, to be described by the legal subdivisions of the public-land surveys, or if unsurveyed, to be surveyed by the United States, at the expense of the applicant, in accordance with regulations to be prescribed by the Secretary of the Interior. Leases may be for indeterminate periods, upon such conditions as may be imposed by the Secretary of the Interior, including covenants relative to methods of mining, prevention of waste, and productive development. For the privilege of mining, extracting, and disposing of the oil or other minerals covered by a lease under this section the lessee shall pay to the United States such royalties as shall be specified in the lease and an annual rental, payable at the beginning of each year, at the rate of 50 cents per acre per annum, for the lands, included in the lease, the rental paid for any one year to be credited against the royalties accruing for that year; such royalties to be subject to readjustment at the end of each twenty-year period by the Secretary of the Interior: *Provided,* That for the purpose of encouraging the production of petroleum products from shales the Secretary may, in his discretion, waive the payment of any royalties and rental during the first five years of any lease; *Provided,* That any person having a valid claim to such minerals under existing laws on January 1, 1919, shall, upon the relinquishment of such claim, be entitled to a lease under the provisions of this section for such area of the land relinquished as shall not exceed the maximum area authorized by this section to be leased to an individual or corporation: *Provided, however,* That no claimant for a lease who has been guilty of any fraud or who had knowledge or reasonable grounds to know of any fraud, or who has not acted honestly and in good faith, shall be entitled to any of the benefits of this section: *Provided further,* That not more than one lease shall be granted under this section to any one person, association, or corporation.

ALASKA OIL PROVISO

Sec. 22. That any bona fide occupant or claimant of oil or gas bearing lands in the Territory of Alaska, who, or whose predecessors in interest, prior to withdrawal had complied otherwise with the requirements of the mining laws, but had made no discovery of oil or gas in wells and who prior to withdrawal had made substantial improvements for the discovery of oil or gas on or for each location or had prior to the passage of this Act expended not less than $250 in improvements on or for each location shall be entitled, upon relinquishment or surrender to the United States within one year from the date of this Act, or within six months after denial or withdrawal of application for patent, to a prospecting permit or permits, lease or leases, under this Act covering such lands, not exceding five permits or leases in number and not exceeding an aggregate of one thousand two hundred and eighty acres each: *Provided,* That leases in Alaska under this Act whether as a result of prospecting permits or otherwise shall be upon such rental and royalties as shall be fixed by the Secretary of the Interior and specified in the lease, and be subject to readjustment at the end of each twenty-year period of the lease: *Provided further,* That for the purpose of encouraging the production of petroleum products in Alaska the Secretary may, in his discretion, waive the payment of any rental or royalties not exceeding the first five years of any lease.

No claimant for a lease who has been guilty of any fraud or who had knowledge or reasonable grounds to know of any fraud, or who has not acted honestly and in good faith, shall be entitled to any of the benefits of this section.

SODIUM

Sec. 23. That the Secretary of the Interior is hereby authorized and directed, under such rules and regulations as he may prescribe, to grant to any qualified applicant a prospecting permit which shall give the exclusive right to prospect for chlorides, sulphates, carbonates, borates, silicates, or nitrates of sodium dissolved in and soluble in water, and accumulated by concentration, in lands belonging to the United States for a period of not exceeding two years;

Provided, That the area to be included in such a permit shall be not exceeding two thousand five hundred and sixty acres of land in reasonably compact form: *Provided further,* That the provisions of this section shall not apply to lands in San Bernardino County, California.

Sec. 24. That upon showing to the satisfaction of the Secretary of the Interior that valuable deposits of one of the substances enumerated in section 23 hereof has been discovered by the permittee within the area covered by his permit and that such land is chiefly valuable therefor the permittee shall be entitled to a lease for one-half of the land embraced in the prospecting permit, at a royalty of not less than one-eighth of the amount or value of the production, to be taken and described by legal subdivisions of the public-land surveys, or if the land be not surveyed by survey executed at the cost of the permittee in accordance with the rules and regulations to be prescribed by the Secretary of the Interior. The permittee shall also have the preference right to lease the remainder of the lands embraced within the limits of his permit at a royalty of not less than one-eighth of the amount or value of the production to be fixed by the Secretary of the Interior. Lands known to contain such valuable deposits as are enumerated in section 23 hereof and not covered by permits or leases, except such lands as are situated in said county of San Bernardino, shall be held subject to lease, and may be leased by the Secretary of the Interior through advertisement, competitive bidding, or such other methods as he may by general regulations adopt, and in such areas as he shall fix, not exceeding two thousand five hundred and sixty acres; all leases to be conditioned upon the payment by the lessee of such royalty of not less than one-eighth of the amount or value of the production as may be fixed in the lease, and the payment in advance of a rental of 50 cents per acre for the first calendar year or fraction thereof and $1 per acre per annum thereafter during the continuance of the lease, the rental paid for any one year to be credited on the royalty for that year. Leases may be for indeterminate periods, subject to readjustment at the end of each twenty-year period, upon such conditions not inconsistent herewith as may be incorporated in each lease or prescribed in general regulation theretofore issued by the Secretary of the Interior, including covenants relative to mining methods, waste, period of preliminary development, and minimum production, and a lessee under this section may be lessee of the remaining lands in his permit.

Sec. 25. That in addition to areas of such mineral land which may be included in any such prospecting permits or leases, the Secretary of the Interior, in his discretion, may grant to a permittee or lessee of lands containing sodium deposits, and subject to the payment of an annual rental of not less than 25 cents per acre, the exclusive right to use, during the life of the permit or lease, a tract of unoccupied nonmineral public land, not exceeding forty acres in area, for camp sites, refining works, and other purposes connected with and necessary to the proper development and use of the deposits covered by the permit or lease.

GENERAL PROVISIONS APPLICABLE TO COAL, PHOSPHATES, SODIUM, OIL, OIL SHALE, AND GAS LEASES

Sec. 26. That the Secretary of the Interior shall reserve and may exercise the authority to cancel any prospecting permit upon failure by the permittee to exercise due diligence in the prosecution of the prospecting work in accordance with the terms and conditions stated in the permit, and shall insert in every such permit issued under the provisions of this Act appropriate provisions for its concellation by him.

Sec. 27. That no person, association, or corporation, except as herein provided, shall take or hold more than one coal, phosphate, or sodium lease during the life of such lease in any one State; no person, association, or corporation shall take or hold, at one time, more than three oil or gas leases granted hereunder in any one State, and not more than one lease within the geologic structure of the same producing oil or gas field; no corporation shall hold any interest as a stockholder of another corporation in more than such number of leases; and no person or corporation shall take or hold any interest or interests as a member of an association or associations or as a stockholder of a corporation or corporations holding a lease under the provisions hereof, which, together with the area embraced in any direct holding of a lease under this Act, or which, together with any other interest or interests, as a member of an association or associations or as a stockholder of a coporation or corporations holding a lease under the provisions hereof, for any kind of mineral leased hereunder, exceeds in the aggregate an amount equivalent to the maximum number of acres of the respective kinds of minerals allowed to any one lessee under this Act. Any interests held in violation of this Act shall be forfeited to the United States by appropriate proceedings instituted by the Attorney General for that purpose in the United States district court for the district in which the property or some part thereof, is located, except that any ownership or interest forbidden in this Act which may be acquired by descent, will, judgment, or decree may be held for two years and not longer after its acquisition: *Provided,* That nothing herein contained shall be construed to limit sections 18, 18-a, 19, and 22 or to prevent any number of lessees under the provisions of this Act from combining their several interests so far as may be necessary for the purposes of constructing and carrying on the business of a refinery, or of establishing and constructing as a common carrier a pipe line or lines of railroads to be operated and used by them jointly in the transportation of oil from their several wells, or from the wells of other lessees under this Act, or the transportation of coal: *Provided further,* That any combination for such purpose or purposes shall be subject to the approval of the Secretary of the Interior on application to him for permission to form the same: *And provided further,* That if any of the lands or deposits leased under the provisions of this Act shall be subleased, trusteed, possessed, or controlled by any devise permanently, temporarily, directly, indirectly, tacitly, or in any manner whatsoever, so that they form the part of, or are in anywise controlled by, any combination in the form of an unlawful trust, with consent of lessee, or form the subject of any contract or conspiracy in restraint of trade in the mining or selling of coal, phosphate, oil, oil shale, gas, or sodium entered into by the lessee, or any agreement or understanding written, verbal or otherwise to which such lessee shall be a party, of which his or its output is to be or become the subject, to control the price or prices thereof or of any holding of such lands by any individual, partnership, association, corporation, or control, in excess of the amounts of lands provided in this Act, the lease thereof shall be forfeited by appropriate court proceedings.

Sec. 28. That rights of way through the public lands, including the forest reserves, of the United States are hereby granted for pipe line purposes for the transportation of oil or natural gas to any applicant possessing the qualifications provided in section 1 of this Act, to the extent of the ground occupied by the said pipe line and twenty-five feet on each side of the same under such regulations as to survey, location, application, and use as may be prescribed by the Secretary of the Interior and upon the express condition that such pipe lines shall be constructed, operated, and maintained as common carriers: *Provided*, That the Government shall in express terms reserve and shall provide in every lease of oil lands hereunder that the lessee, assignee, or beneficiary, if owner, or operator or owner of the controlling interest in any pipe line or of any company operating the same which may be operated accessible to the oil derived from under such lease, shall at reasonable rates and without discrimination accept and convey the oil of the Government or of any citizen or company not the owner of any pipe line, operating a lease or purchasing gas or oil under the provisions of this Act: *Provided further*, That no right of way shall hereafter be granted over said lands for the transportation of oil or natural gas except under and subject to the provisions, limitations, and conditions of this section. Failure to comply with the provisions of this section or the regulations prescribed by the Secretary of the Interior shall be ground for forfeiture of the grant by the United States district court for the district in which the property, or some part thereof is located in an appropriate proceeding.

Sec. 29. That any permit, lease, occupation, or use permitted under this Act shall reserve to the Secretary of the Interior the right to permit upon such terms as he may determine to be just, for joint or several use, such easements or rights of way, including easements in tunnels upon, through, or in the lands leased, occupied, or used as may be necessary or appropriate to the working of the same, or of other lands containing the deposits described in this Act, and the treatment and shipment of the products thereof by or under authority of the Government, its lessees, or permittees, and for other public purposes: *Provided*, That said Secretary, in his discretion, in making any lease under this Act, may reserve to the United States the right to lease, sell, or otherwise dispose of the surface of the lands embraced within such lease under existing law or laws hereafter enacted, in so far as said surface is not necessary for use of the lessee in extracting and removing the deposits therein: *Provided fur-*

ther, That if such reservation is made it shall be so determined before the offering of such lease: *And provided further*, That the said Secretary, during the life of the lease, is authorized to issue such permits for easements herein provided to be reserved.

Sec. 30. That no lease issued under the authority of this Act shall be assigned or sublet, except with the consent of the Secretary of the Interior. The lessee may, in the discretion of the Secretary of the Interior, be permitted at any time to make written relinquishment of all rights under such a lease, and upon acceptance thereof be thereby relieved of all future obligations under said lease, and may with like consent surrender any legal subdivision of the area included within the lease. Each lease shall contain provisions for the purpose of insuring the exercise of reasonable diligence, skill, and care in the operaton of said property; a provision that such rules for the safety and welfare of the miners and for the prevention of undue waste as may be prescribed by said Secretary shall be observed, including a restriction of the workday to not exceeding eight hours in any one day for underground workers except in cases of emergency; provisions prohibiting the employment of any boy under the age of sixteen or the employment of any girl or woman, without regard to age, in any mine below the surface; provisions securing the workmen complete freedom of purchase; provision requiring the payment of wages at least twice a month in lawful money of the United States, and providing proper rules and regulations to insure the fair and just weighing and measurement of the coal mined by each miner, and such other provisions as he may deem necessary to insure the sale of the production of such leased lands to the United States and to the public at reasonable prices, for the protection of the interests of the United States, for the prevention of monopoly, and for the safeguarding of the public welfare: *Provided*, That none of such provisions shall be in conflict with the laws of the State in which the leased property is situated.

Sec 31. That any lease issued under the provisions of this Act may be forfeited and cancelled by an appropriate proceeding in the United States district court for the district in which the property, or some part thereof is located whenever the lessee fails to comply with any of the provisions of this Act, of the lease, or of the general regulations promulgated under this Act and in force at the date of the lease; and the lease may provide for resort to appropriate methods for the settlement of disputes or for remedies for breach of specified conditions thereof.

Sec. 32. That the Secretary of the Interior is authorized to prescribe necessary and proper rules and regulations and to do any and all things necessary to carry out and accomplish the purposes of this Act, also to fix and determine the boundary lines of any structure, or oil or gas field, for the purposes of this Act: *Provided*, That nothing in this Act shall be construed or held to affect the rights of the States or other local authority to exercise any rights which they may have, including the right to levy and collect taxes upon improvements, output or mines, or other rights, property, or assets of any lessee of the United States.

Sec. 33. That all statements, representations, or reports required by the Secretary of the Interior under this Act shall be upon oath, unless otherwise specified by him, and in such form and upon such blanks as the Secretary of the Interior may require.

Sec. 34. That all provisions of this Act shall also apply to all deposits of coal, phosphate, sodium, oil, oil shale, or gas in the lands of the United States, which lands may have been or may be disposed of under laws reserving to the United States such deposits, with the right to prospect for, mine, and remove the same, subject to such conditions as are or may hereafter be provided by such laws reserving such deposits.

Sec. 35. That 10 per centum of all money received from sales, bonuses, royalties, and rentals under the provisions of this Act excepting those from Alaska, shall be paid into the Treasury of the United States and credited to miscellaneous receipts; for past production 70 per centum, and for future production 52½ per centum of the amounts derived from such bonuses, royalties, and rentals shall be paid into, reserved, and appropriated as a part of the reclamation fund created by the Act of Congress, known as the Reclamation Act, approved June 17, 1902, and for past production 20 per centum, and for future production 37½ per centum of the amounts derived from such bonuses, royalties, and rentals shall be paid by the Secretary of the Treasury after the expiration of each fiscal year to the State within the boundaries of which the leased lands or deposits are or were located, said moneys to be used by such State or subdivisions thereof for the construction and maintenance of public roads or for the support of public schools or other public educational institutions, as the legislature of the State may direct: *Provided,* That all moneys which may accrue to the United States under the provisions of this Act from lands within the naval petroleum reserves shall be deposited in the Treasury as "Miscellaneous receipts."

Sec. 36. That all royalty accruing to the United States under any oil or gas lease or permit under this Act on demand of the Secretary of the Interior shall be paid in oil or gas.

Upon granting any oil or gas lease under this Act, and from time to time thereafter during said lease, the Secretary of the Interior shall, except whenever in his judgment it is desirable to retain the same for the use of the United States, offer for sale for such period as he may determine, upon notice and advertisement on sealed bids or at public auction, all royalty oil and gas accruing or reserved to the United States under such lease. Such advertisement and sale shall reserve to the Secretary of the Interior the right to reject all bids whenever within his judgment the interest of the United States demands, and in cases where no satisfactory bid is received or where the accepted bidder fails to complete the purchase, or where the Secretary of the Interior shall determine that it is unwise in the public interest to accept the offer of the highest bidder, the Secretary of the Interior, within his discretion, may readvertise such royalty for sale, or sell at private sale at not less than the market price for such period, or accept the value thereof from the lessee: *Provided, however,* That pending the making of a permanent contract for the sale of any royalty, oil or gas as herein provided, the

Secretary of the Interior may sell the current product at private sale, at not less than the market price: *And provided further,* That any royalty, oil, or gas may be sold at not less than the market price at private sale to any department or agency of the United States.

Sec. 37. That the deposits of coal, phosphate, sodium, oil, oil shale, and gas, herein referred to, in lands valuable for such minerals, including lands and deposits described in the joint resolution entitled "Joint resolution authorizing the Secretary of the Interior to permit the continuation of coal mining operations on certain lands in Wyoming," approved August 1, 1912 (Thirty-seventh Statutes at Large, page 1346), shall be subject to disposition only in the form and manner provided in this Act, except as to valid claims existent at date of the passage of this Act and thereafter maintained in compliance with the laws under which initiated, which claims may be perfected under such laws, including discovery.

Sec. 38. That, until otherwise provided, the Secretary of the Interior, shall be authorized to prescribe fees and commissions to be paid registers and receivers of the United States land offices on account of business transacted under the provisions of this Act.

1920—Act of June 5, 1920 (41 Stat. L., 874, 912)—An Act Making appropriations for sundry civil expenses of the Government for the fiscal year ending June 30, 1921, and for other purposes.

* * * *

Persons employed during the fiscal year 1921 in field work outside of the District of Columbia under the Bureau of Mines may be detailed temporarily for service in the District of Columbia, for purposes of preparing results of their field work: all persons so detailed shall be paid in addition to their regular compensation only their actual traveling expenses or per diem in lieu of subsistence in going to and returning therefrom: *Provided,* That nothing herein shall prevent the payment to employees of the Bureau of Mines of their necessary expenses, or per diem in lieu of subsistence while on temporary detail in the District of Columbia, for purposes only of consultation or investigations on behalf of the United States. All details made hereunder and the purposes of each, during the preceding fiscal year shall be reported in the annual estimates of appropriations to Congress at the beginning of each regular session thereof;

Government fuel yards: For the purchase and transportation of fuel; storing and handling of fuel in yards; maintenance and operation of yards and equipment, including motor-propelled passenger-carrying vehicles for inspectors, purchase of equipment, rentals, and all other expenses requisite for and incident thereto, including personal services in the District of Columbia, the unexpended balance of the appropriation made for these purposes for the fiscal year 1921 is reappropriated and made available for such purposes for the fiscal year 1922, and of such sum not exceeding $500 shall be available to settle claims for damages caused to private property by motor vehicles used in delivering fuel: *Provided,* That all moneys received from the sales of fuel during the fiscal year 1922 shall be credited to this appropriation and be available for the purposes of this paragraph;

Hereafter the Secretary of the Interior may have sand, gravel, stone, and other material hauled for the municipal government of the District of Columbia, and for branches of the Federal service in the District of Columbia, whenever it may be practicable and economical to have such work performed by using trucks of the Government fuel yard not needed at the time for the hauling of fuel. Payment for such work shall be made on the basis of the actual cost to the Government fuel yards;

Hereafter the Secretary of the Interior is authorized to deliver during the months of April, May, and June of each year, to all branches of the Federal service and the municipal government in the District of Columbia, such quantities of fuel for their use during the following fiscal year as it may be practicable to store at the points of consumption, payment therefor to be made by these branches of the Federal service and municipal government from their applicable appropriations for such fiscal year;

During the fiscal year 1921, the head of any department or independent establishment of the Government having funds available for scientific investigations and requiring coöperative work by the Bureau of Mines on scientific investigations within the scope of the functions of that bureau and which it is unable to perform within the limits of its appropriations, may, with the approval of the Secretary of the Interior, transfer to the Bureau of Mines such sums as may be necessary to carry on such investigations. The Secretary of the Treasury shall transfer on the books of the Treasury Department any sums which may be authorized hereunder and such amounts shall be placed to the credit of the Bureau of Mines for the performance of work for the department or establishment from which the transfer is made.

1921—Act of March 4, 1921 (41 Stat. L., 1367, 1400)—An Act Making appropriations for sundry civil expenses of the Government for the fiscal year ending June 30, 1922, and for other purposes.

That the following sums are appropriated, out of any money in the Treasury not otherwise appropriated, for the fiscal year ending June 30, 1921, namely:

* * * *

BUREAU OF MINES

For general expenses, including pay of the director and necessary assistants, clerks, and other employees, in the office in the District of Columbia, and in the field, and every other expense requisite for and incident to the general work of the bureau in the District of Columbia, and in the field, to be expended under the direction of the Secretary of the Interior, $76,900;

For investigations as to the causes of mine explosions, methods of mining, especially in relation to the safety of miners, the appliances best adapted to prevent accidents, the possible improvement of conditions under which mining operations are carried on, the use of explosives and electricity, the prevention of accidents, and other inquiries and technologic investigations pertinent to the mining industry, and including all equipment, supplies, and expenses of travel and subsistence, and for the erection of a garage for mine-rescue truck at Norton, Virginia; $409,065;

For investigation of mineral fuels and unfinished mineral products belonging to or for the use of the United States, with a view to their most efficient mining, preparation, treatment, and use, and to recommend to various departments such changes in selection and use of fuel as may result in greater economy, and including all equipment, supplies, and expenses of travel and subsistence, $142,510;

For inquiries and scientific and technologic investigations concerning the mining, preparation, treatment, and utilization of ores and other mineral substances, with a view to improving health conditions and increasing safety, efficiency, economic development, and conserving resources through the prevention of waste in the mining, quarrying, metallurgical, and other mineral industries; to inquire into the economic conditions affecting these industries; and including all equipment, supplies, expenses of travel and subsistence: *Provided,* That no part thereof may be used for investigation in behalf of any private party, $125,000;

For inquiries and investigations concerning the mining, preparation, treatment, and utilization of petroleum and natural gas, with a view to economic development and conserving resources through the prevention of waste; to inquire into the economic conditions affecting the industry, including equipment, supplies, and expenses of travel and subsistence, $135,000:

Not exceeding 20 per centum of the preceding sums for investigation as to the causes of mine explosions; for inquiries and scientific and technologic investigations concerning the mining, preparation, treatment, and utilization of ores and other mineral substances; for inquiries and investigations concerning the mining, preparation, treatment, and utilization of petroleum and natural gas; and not exceeding 30 per centum of the preceding sums for investigation of mineral fuels and unfinished mineral products belonging to or for the use of the United States may be used during the fiscal year 1922 for personal service in the District of Columbia;

The Secretary of the Treasury may detail medical officers of the Public Health Service for coöperative health, safety, or sanitation work with the Bureau of Mines, and the compensation and expenses of the officers so detailed may be paid from the applicable appropriations made herein for the Bureau of Mines;

For the employment of personal services and all other expenses in connection with the establishment, maintenance, and operation of mining experiment stations, authorized by the Act approved March 3, 1915, $200,000;

For care and maintenance of the buildings and grounds at Pittsburgh, Pennsylvania, including personal services, the operation, maintenance, and repair of passenger automobiles for official use, and all other expenses requisite for and incident thereto, $50,000;

For operation of mine-rescue cars, including personal services, traveling expenses and subsistence, equipment and supplies, authorized by the Act approved March 3, 1915; to be available for expenditure on any preliminary work that may be found necessary in connection with such cars as are to be purchased prior to the time of their actual delivery, $160,000;

For one mine inspector for duty in Alaska, $3,000;

For clerk to mine inspector of Alaska, $1,500;

For per diem, subject to such rules and regulations as the Secretary of the Interior may prescribe, in lieu of subsistence, at a rate not exceeding $4 when absent on official business from his designated headquarters, and for actual necessary traveling and contingent expenses of said inspector and clerk, $2,825;

For technical and scientific books and publications and books of reference, $1,500;

* * * *

In all, Bureau of Mines, $1,439,300.

1921—Act of March 4, 1921 (41 Stat. L., 1444, 1445)—An Act To amend an Act entitled "An Act to codify, revise, and amend the penal laws of the United States," approved March 4, 1909 (Thirty-fifth Statutes at Large, page 1134).

* * * *

Sec. 233. . . . In the execution of the provisions of the Act [as to transportation of explosives] the Interstate Commerce Commission may utilize the services of the bureau for the safe transportation of explosives and other dangerous articles, and may avail itself of the advice and assistance of any department, commission, or board of the Government, but no official or employee of the United States shall receive any additional compensation for such service except as now permitted by law.

1921—Act of June 16, 1921 (Pub. No. 18, 67th Congress)— An Act Making appropriations to supply deficiencies in appropriations for the fiscal year ending June 30, 1921, and prior fiscal years, and for other purposes.

* * * *

BUREAU OF MINES

For inquiries and scientific and technologic investigations concerning the mining, preparation, treatment, and utilization of heavy clay products, cement, feldspar, slate, and other nonmetallics; including all equipment, supplies, expenses of travel and subsistence; fiscal year 1922, $35,000; *Provided,* That no part thereof may be used for investgation in behalf of any private party.

APPENDIX 6

FINANCIAL STATEMENTS

Explanatory Note

Statements showing appropriations, receipts, expenditures, and other financial data for a series of years constitute the most effective single means of exhibiting the growth and development of a service. Due to the fact that Congress has adopted no uniform plan of appropriations for the several services and that the latter employ no uniform plan in respect to the recording and reporting of their receipts and expenditures, it is impossible to present data of this character according to any standard scheme of presentation. In the case of some services the administrative reports contain tables showing financial conditions and operations of the service in considerable detail; in others financial data are almost wholly lacking. Careful study has in all cases been made of such data as are available, and the effort has been made to present the results in such a form as will exhibit the financial operations of the service in the most effective way that circumstances permit.

Appropriations. While the Bureau of Mines receives appropriations from Congress in its own name, it also benefits from appropriations for the Department of the Interior which are either specifically designated for the sole use of the bureau, designed for allotment among the various branches of the department, or made applicable for departmental "overhead" expenses, such as rent, light, stationery, etc. In common with the other branches of the national organization the bureau has benefited from the use of new buildings constructed out of funds provided in appropriations for the Treasury Department. During the war the bureau received appropriations out of general funds appropriated subject to allotment. In the following table, unless otherwise indicated, only those appropriations are included which are specifically stated to be for the sole use of the Bureau of Mines. It includes all deficiency appropriations excepting those items known as "auditors' certified claims." These are usually small, and in most cases their inclusion would involve duplication. To prevent duplication also, reappropriations of unexpended balances have been indicated in footnotes and not included in the body of the statement.

Expenditures. For the fiscal years 1911 to 1918, inclusive the expenditures listed in the following statements are figured on the accrual basis. That is, the amount given as expended out of a specific appropriation represents the total expenditure out of that appropriation regardless of whether the money was expended during the current fiscal year or during the two succeeding years in which the money was available. The expenditures for 1919 and 1920 are figured on a cash basis, and therefore, represent the amounts expended out of the various appropriations during the current fiscal years only. The total of the expenditures for 1918 is somewhat increased by the inclusion of the expenditures on account of the various war allotments.

Repayments. For all work done for other branches of the national government, the Bureau of Mines receives "repayments" or credit items applied to the appropriation accounts to which the respective activities were charged. Such repayments are available for re-expenditure by the bureau for the duration of the original appropriation.

Miscellaneous Receipts. Since 1912 the bureau has been authorized to charge and collect a reasonable fee covering the necessary expenses for tests or investigations authorized by the Secretary of the Interior, other than those performed for the government of the United States or a state government, such fees being charged according to a schedule prepared by the Director of the Bureau and approved by the Secretary and collections being paid into the Treasury to the credit of miscellaneous receipts. Under the act of October 20, 1914 (38 Stat. L., 741) the bureau supervises coal mining operations on leased government lands in Alaska. Under the act of February 25, 1920 (41 Stat. L., 437) the bureau supervises mining operations with reference to coal, oil, gas, etc., on leased government lands and calculates royalties due the Government as the result of such operations. The royalties received under these acts, however, are paid into the Receivers of Public Moneys of the local land offices, under the jurisdiction of the General Land Office.

FINANCIAL STATEMENTS

BUREAU OF MINES
APPROPRIATIONS AND EXPENDITURES: FISCAL YEARS, 1911 TO 1922, INCLUSIVE

Object	Appropriation 1911	Expenditure 1911	Appropriation 1912	Expenditure 1912	Appropriation 1913	Expenditure 1913	Appropriation 1914	Expenditure 1914
Mining experiment stations								
Laboratories, Washington, removal and reinstallation								281.69
Laboratories, Pittsburgh, building	14,700.00	14,700.00			2,000.00	b 1,706.44	c	
Laboratories, Pittsburgh, equipment								
Laboratories, Pittsburgh, removal and reinstallation								
Laboratories, Pittsburgh, removal and improvements								
Laboratories, Pittsburgh, care and maintenance								
Mines in Alaska, inspection								
Mine leases on public domain, administration								
Government fuel yard, establishment	d 8,500.00	3,247.20	d 9,500.00	7,471.92	6,500.00	5,041.05	6,500.00	6,049.30
Government fuel yard, operation and purchase of fuel								
Explosives, regulation								
War materials, investigation								
War minerals, relief fund								
Gas investigation, War Department								
Gas investigation, Navy Department								
Balloon gases								
Carbide furnace, investigation								
Oxygen apparatus, experiments								
Military gas plant								
War minerals								
Totals	$492,200.00	$485,906.04	$475,500.00	$472,928.18	$585,100.00	$581,992.57	$662,000.00	$657,628.44

APPROPRIATIONS AND EXPENDITURES: FISCAL YEARS, 1911 TO 1922, INCLUSIVE—Continued

Object	1911 Appropriation	1911 Expenditure	1912 Appropriation	1912 Expenditure	1913 Appropriation	1913 Expenditure	1914 Appropriation	1914 Expenditure
General expense (principally central office salaries)	$54,000.00	$53,840.23	$54,000.00	$53,893.92	$66,100.00	$65,912.56	$70,000.00	$69,555.35
Reports, publication	5,000.00	4,306.26	....	....	....	....	....	....
Books and publications, purchase	....	....	2,000.00	1,933.62	1,500.00	1,491.67	1,500.00	1,452.91
Increase of compensation	....	....	....	....	....	....	....	....
Mine accidents, investigation	310,000.00	309,892.13	310,000.00	309,866.97	320,000.00	319,700.51	347,000.00	346,364.95
Mine-rescue station, McAlester, purchase of land and building	....	....	....	....	....	....	....	....
Mine-rescue station, McAlester, repairs	....	....	....	....	....	....	....	....
Mine-rescue station, Birmingham, extension and equipment	....	....	....	....	....	....	....	....
Mine-rescue equipment and supplies	....	....	....	....	....	....	....	....
Land for mine-rescue cars, purchase or lease	....	....	....	....	[a]4,000.00	3,344.23	2,000.00	37.45
Mine-rescue cars, purchase	....	....	....	....	....	....	....	....
Mine-rescue cars, equipment	....	....	....	....	....	....	....	....
Mine-rescue cars, operation	....	....	....	....	50,000.00	49,962.45	100,000.00	99,514.13
Mine-rescue cars, reconstruction and repair	....	....	....	....	....	....	....	....
Mining, treatment and utilization of minerals, investigation	....	....	....	....	....	....	....	....
Mining, treatment and utilization of non-metallic minerals, investigation	....	....	....	....	....	....	....	....
Fuels, testing	100,000.00	99,920.22	100,000.00	99,761.75	135,000.00	134,833.66	135,000.00	134,372.66
Lignite and peat, investigation	....	....	....	....	....	....	....	....
Petroleum and natural gas, investigation	....	....	....	....	....	....	....	....

[a] Available until expended.
[b] Figured on a cash basis.
[c] Balance from 1913 available.
[d] Includes inspection of mines in New Mexico.

FINANCIAL STATEMENTS

APPROPRIATIONS AND EXPENDITURES: FISCAL YEARS 1911 TO 1922, INCLUSIVE—*Continued.*

Object	Appropriation 1915	Expenditure	Appropriation 1916	Expenditure	Appropriation 1917	Expenditure	Appropriation 1918	Expenditure
General expenses, principally central office salaries	$70,000.00	$69,697.85	$70,000.00	$69,669.20	$70,000.00	$69,046.27	$73,300.00	$72,982.67
Reports, publication	....	....	....	....	....	....	....	....
Books and publications, purchase	1,500.00	1,445.34	1,500.00	1,219.49	1,500.00	1,496.90	1,500.00	1,462.24
Increase of compensation	....	....	....	....	....	....	25,065.11	25,065.11
Mine accidents, investigation	347,000.00	346,001.86	374,000.00	344,409.80	347,000.00	344,421.20	353,800.00	344,453.16
Mine-rescue station, McAlester, purchase of land and building	5,500.00	5,500.00	....	....	....	....	....	....
Mine-rescue station, McAlester, repairs	....	....	500.00	496.00	....	....	....	....
Mine-rescue station, Birmingham, extension and equipment	....	....	3,000.00	3,996.37	....	....	....	....
Mine-rescue equipment and supplies	30,000.00	29,800.67	....	....	....	....	....	....
Land for mine-rescue cars, purchase or lease	1,000.00	36.00	1,000.00	36.00	1,000.00	274.55	1,000.00	279.65
Mine-rescue cars, purchase	....	....	....	....	53,000.00	52,998.00	81,750.00	81,644.10
Mine-rescue cars, equipment	....	....	....	....	13,500.00	13,500.00	13,500.00	13,363.94
Mine-rescue cars, operation	....	....	....	....	35,000.00	31,412.76	98,000.00	78,929.92
Mine-rescue cars, reconstruction and repair	....	....	....	....	26,055.00	25,706.72	....	....
Mining, treatment and utilization of minerals, investigation	100,000.00	99,506.16	100,000.00	99,708.22	100,000.00	98,161.95	100,000.00	98,217.86
Mining, treatment and utilization of non-metallic minerals, investigation	....	....	....	....	....	....	....	....
Fuels, testing	135,000.00	134,880.54	135,000.00	133,830.22	135,000.00	134,893.00	135,000.00	128,057.87
Lignite and peat, investigation	....	....	....	....	....	....	....	....
Petroleum and natural gas, investigation	25,000.00	24,866.14	35,000.00	34,943.49	70,000.00	69,702.10	100,000.00	98,106.54

THE BUREAU OF MINES

APPROPRIATIONS AND EXPENDITURES: FISCAL YEARS 1911 TO 1922, INCLUSIVE—*Continued.*

Object	Appropriation 1915	Expenditure 1915	Appropriation 1916	Expenditure 1916	Appropriation 1917	Expenditure 1917	Appropriation 1918	Expenditure 1918
Mining experiment stations	....	....	....	....	75,000.00	74,348.37	150,000.00	149,004.46
Laboratories, Washington, removal and reinstallation	....	....	....	....	....	....	....	....
Laboratories, Pittsburgh, building	500,000.00	[a]	350,000.00	....	....	....	....	....
Laboratories, Pittsburgh, equipment	10,000.00	9,994.57	....	....	....	....	....	....
Laboratories, Pittsburgh, removal and reinstallation	....	....	57,300.00	[b] 10,531.19	[c] 42,700.00	[b] 39,444.29	[d]	[b] 39,444.29
Laboratories, Pittsburgh, removal and improvements	....	....	....	....	35,000.00	....	[e]	[b] 15,164.31
Laboratories, Pittsburgh, care and maintenance	....	....	....	....	4,305.00	12.00	17,220.00	13,693.92
Mines in Alaska, inspection	5,500.00	4,600.00	7,000.00	5,681.94	7,000.00	4,806.08	7,000.00	5,621.37
Mine leases on public domain, administration	....	....	....	....	....	....	....	....
Explosives, regulation	....	....	....	....	....	....	....	....
Government fuel yard, establishment	....	....	....	....	....	....	[f] 300,000.00	[b] 205,641.91
Government fuel yard, operation and purchase of fuel	....	....	....	....	....	....	....	....
War materials, investigation	....	....	....	....	....	....	150,000.00	[b] 17,824.35
War minerals, relief fund	....	....	....	....	....	....	....	....
Gas investigations, War Department [g]	....	....	....	....	....	....	2,212,000.00	[o]2,208,143.60
Gas investigations, Navy Department [h]	....	....	....	....	....	....	250,000.00	[b] 249,229.31
Balloon gases [g] and [h]	....	....	....	....	....	....	247,000.00	[b] 236,214.96
Carbide furnace investigation [g]	....	....	....	....	....	....	3,000.00	[b] 553.15
Oxygen apparatus, experiments [g]	....	....	....	....	....	....	100,000.00	[b] 66,122.50
Military gas plant [g]	....	....	....	....	....	....	250,000.00	[b] 27,330.49
War minerals	....	....	....	....	....	....	....	....
Totals	$1,230,500.00	$726,329.48	$1,107,300.00	$702,521.92	$1,029,560.00	$960,224.19	$4,669,135.11	$4,176,561.68

[a] Appropriated under Supervising Architect of the Treasury and money expended by him.
[b] Figured on a cash basis.
[c] In addition, balance from 1916 reappropriated.
[d] Balance from 1916 and 1917 reappropriated.
[e] Balance from 1917 available in 1918.
[f] Available until expended.
[g] Transferred from War Department appropriations.
[h] Transferred from Navy Department appropriations.

FINANCIAL STATEMENTS

APPROPRIATIONS AND EXPENDITURES: FISCAL YEARS 1911 TO 1922 INCLUSIVE—*Continued*.

Object	Appropriation 1919	Expenditure	Appropriation 1920	Expenditure	Appropriation 1921	Expenditure	Appropriation 1922	Expenditure
General expense (principally central office salaries)	$73,300.00	$71,177.85	$73,300.00	$72,894.00	$76,900.00	$76,900.00	$76,900.00	
Reports, publication								
Books and publications, purchase	1,500.00	1,451.04	1,500.00	1,500.00	1,500.00	1,500.00	1,500.00	
Increase of compensation	63,960.93	63,960.93	126,807.02	126,807.02	119,502.22			
Mine accidents, investigation	387,210.00	390,436.83	422,210.00	428,001.16	409,065.00	409,065.00	409,065.00	
Mine-rescue station, McAlester, purchase of land and building								
Mine-rescue station, McAlester, repairs								
Mine-rescue station, Birmingham, extension and equipment								
Mine-rescue equipment and supplies								
Land for mine-rescue cars, purchase or lease	1,000.00	419.58	1,000.00	307.06	1,000.00			
Mine-rescue cars, purchase								
Mine-rescue cars, equipment								
Mine-rescue cars, operation	136,667.00	97,528.65	154,667.00	153,486.13	154,667.00	153,486.13	160,000.00	
Mine-rescue cars, reconstruction and repair								
Mining, treatment and utilization of minerals, investigation	100,000.00	95,022.49	100,000.00	99,640.89	125,000.00		125,000.00	
Mining, treatment and utilization of non-metallic minerals, investigation								
Fuels, testing	135,000.00	134,444.58	150,000.00	153,763.06			35,000.00	
Lignite and peat, investigation	a 100,000.00	2,984.11		13,484.85	142,510.00	142,510.00	142,510.00	
Petroleum and natural gas, investigation	100,000.00	107,046.69	125,000.00	124,939.36	135,000.00	135,000.00	135,000.00	

APPROPRIATIONS AND EXPENDITURES: FISCAL YEARS, 1911 TO 1922, INCLUSIVE—Continued

Object	Appropriation 1919	Expenditure	Appropriation 1920	Expenditure	Appropriation 1921	Expenditure	Appropriation 1922	Expenditure
Mining experiment stations	150,000.00	150,630.91	150,000.00	149,796.27	200,000.00		200,000.00	
Laboratories, Washington, removal and reinstallation								
Laboratories, Pittsburgh, building								
Laboratories, Pittsburgh, equipment								
Laboratories, Pittsburgh, removal and reinstallation	b	21,224.47						
Laboratories, Pittsburgh, removal and improvements	c	19,830.52						
Laboratories, Pittsburgh, care and maintenance	17,220.00	16,773.18	17,220.00	17,075.83	50,000.00		50,000.00	
Mines in Alaska, inspection	7,000.00	5,978.77	7,000.00	5,801.10	7,000.00		7,000.00	
Mine leases on public domain, administration			d					
Explosives regulation	300,000.00	269,124.86						
Government fuel yard, establishment	432,300.00	431,960.38		14,161.13	60,000.00		132,000.00	
Government fuel yard, operation and purchase of fuel	1,154,088.00	1,591,901.28	e	1,924,759.57	e		e	
War materials, investigation	e	131,871.57						
War minerals, relief fund	f 8,500,000.00	43,619.17						
Gas investigation, War Department				1,401,302.56				
Gas investigation, Navy Department								
Balloon gas, investigation								
Carbide furnace								
Oxygen apparatus experiments								
Military gas plant	100,000.00							
War minerals g		14,637.72						
Totals	$11,759,245.93	$3,662,025.52	$1,328,704.02	$4,687,719.99	$1,482,144.22		$1,473,975.00	

a Available until expended.
b Balance from 1916 and 1917 reappropriated.
c Balance from 1918 reappropriated.
d All but $15,000 of the previous appropriations returned to the treasury.
e Balance from 1919 reappropriated.
f Included in appropriation for Department of the Interior.
g Included in appropriation for the executive office.

FINANCIAL STATEMENTS 145

MISCELLANEOUS RECEIPTS AND REPAYMENTS
*Miscellaneous Receipts: Fiscal Years 1911 to 1920, Inclusive

On account of	1911	1912	1913	1914	1915
Royalties from coal mines on leased Government lands[a]	$	$	$ 7,594.96	$ 10,205.52	$ 12,492.41
Fees for tests and analyses		6,024.00	1,885.00	1,845.00	4,970.50
Fees for copies of records				2.13	9.30
Sales of publications	976.45	791.95	457.70	946.75	1,540.55
Sales of old or worn out material and equipment					
Totals	$ 976.45	$ 6,815.95	$ 9,907.66	$ 12,999.40	$ 19,012.76

On account of	1916	1917	1918	1919	1920	Total
Royalties from coal mines on leased Government lands[a]	$ 16,680.44	$ 17,350.96	$ 23,446.31	$ 24,075.22	$ 25,584.93	$ 137,630.75
Fees for tests and analyses	4,936.53	3,073.83	470.65	1,383.29	8,579.25	33,138.10
Fees for copies of records	51.53	6.12	17.65	94.45	24.55	205.73
Sales of publications	6,294.50	3,939.92	4,372.60	4,492.40	14,645.70	38,458.52
Sales of old or worn out material and equipment	459.95	1,006.00	3.50	575.00	1,350.79	3,395.24
Totals	$ 28,422.95	$ 25,576.88	$ 28,310.71	$ 30,620.36	$ 50,185.22	$ 212,828.34

Repayments: Fiscal Years 1911 to 1920 Inclusive

Appropriation Credited	1911	1912	1913	1914	1915
General expenses	$ 5,411.18	$ 2,571.97	$ 85.61	$ 1,456.78	$ 1,603.75
Mine accidents, investigation			2,881.11		
Petroleum and natural gas, investigation			108.00		
Mining experiment stations, operation					
Fuels, testing	917.11	977.54			426.11
Government fuel yard, operation and purchase of fuel					
Totals	$ 6,328.29	$ 3,549.51	$ 3,074.72	$ 1,456.78	$ 2,029.86

Appropriation Credited	1916	1917	1918	1919	1920
General expenses	$ 6.00	$ 1,379.80	$ 169.85	$ 4,585.56	$ 6,116.47
Mine accidents, investigation	1,440.00			7,318.82	205.10
Petroleum and natural gas, investigation				912.11	
Mining experiment stations, operation				1,215.55	4,025.81
Fuels, testing				1,536,216.97	1,653,467.90
Government fuel yard, operation and purchase of fuel					
Totals	$ 1,446.00	$ 1,379.80	$ 169.85	$1,550,249.01	$1,663,815.37

*Prepared by the Bureau of Mines. [a] Consists entirely of payments made by the Owl Creek Coal Company, Gebo, Wyoming; the only mines under the administrative supervision of the bureau during the above period.

APPENDIX 7

BIBLIOGRAPHY

BUREAU OF MINES

EXPLANATORY NOTE

The bibliographies appended to the several monographs aim to list only those works which deal directly with the services to which they relate, their history, activities, organization, methods of business, problems, etc. They are intended primarily to meet the needs of those persons who desire to make a further study of the services from an administrative standpoint. They thus do not include the titles of publications of the services themselves, except in so far as they treat of the services, their work and problems. Nor do they include books or articles dealing merely with technical features other than administrative of the work of the services. In a few cases explanatory notes have been appended where it was thought they would aid in making known the character or value of the publication to which they relate.

After the completion of the series the bibliographies may be assembled and separately published as a bibliography of the Administrative Branch of the National Government.

BIBLIOGRAPHIES

U. S. *Bureau of mines.* Fuel efficiency publications of the Bureau of mines. March, 1913. [Washington, Govt. print. off., 1913] 8 p.

―――― ―――― The publications of the Bureau of mines. Nov., 1920. [Washington, Govt. print. off., 1920] 76 p.

―――― *Superintendent of documents.* Mines and mining publications of United States Bureau of mines for sale by the Superintendent of documents, Washington, D. C. [3d ed.] [Washington, Govt. print. off.] 1915. 18 p. (Price list 58-3d ed.)

OFFICIAL PUBLICATIONS

Clark, Harold H. The electrical section of the Bureau of mines, its purpose and equipment. Washington, Govt.

[1] Compiled by M. Alice Matthews.

print. off., 1911. 12 p. (U. S. Bureau of mines. Technical paper 4)

Davis, Joseph D. The fuel-inspection laboratory of the Bureau of mines. (*In* Pope, G. S. Government coal purchases. Washington, 1912. p. 74-91. U. S. Bureau of mines. Bulletin 41)

[Describes equipment and method of procedure used in the laboratory in making a coal analysis. For the use of the layman]

Illinois. *Coal mining investigations (Coöperative agreement)* Bulletin 1- Urbana, University of Illinois, 1913-

[Coöperative agreement between the State geological survey, the Department of mining engineering, University of Illinois, and the U. S. Bureau of mines]

Illinois. *Coal mining investigations (Coöperative agreement).* Preliminary report on organization and method of investigations. Urbana, University of Illinois, 1913. 71 p.

Manning, Van H. Mine safety devices developed by the United States Bureau of mines. *illus.* (In Smithsonian institution. Annual report . . . 1916. Washington, 1917 p. 533-44)

U. S. *Bureau of mines.* Annual report of the director. 1910-11- Washington, Govt. print. off., 1912.

────── Exhibits of United States Bureau of mines in Mines and metallurgy palace, Panama-Pacific international exposition, San Francisco, Cal. n.p., 1915. 15 p.

────── Experiment stations of the Bureau of mines, by Van H. Manning. Washington, Govt. print. off., 1919. 106 p. (*Its* Bulletin, no. 175)

────── Manual of regulations of the Bureau of mines. ₁Washington, Govt. print. off., 1915. 114 p.

────── Report of the conference of state and government officials regarding the standardization of mining statistics and mine regulations, Washington, D. C., February 24 and 25, 1916. Washington, Govt. print. off., 1916. 3-85 p.

[One of the principal objects of the meeting was to bring about a coöperative agreement between the various state organizations and Federal bureaus interested in the collection of statistics relating to the mining industry]

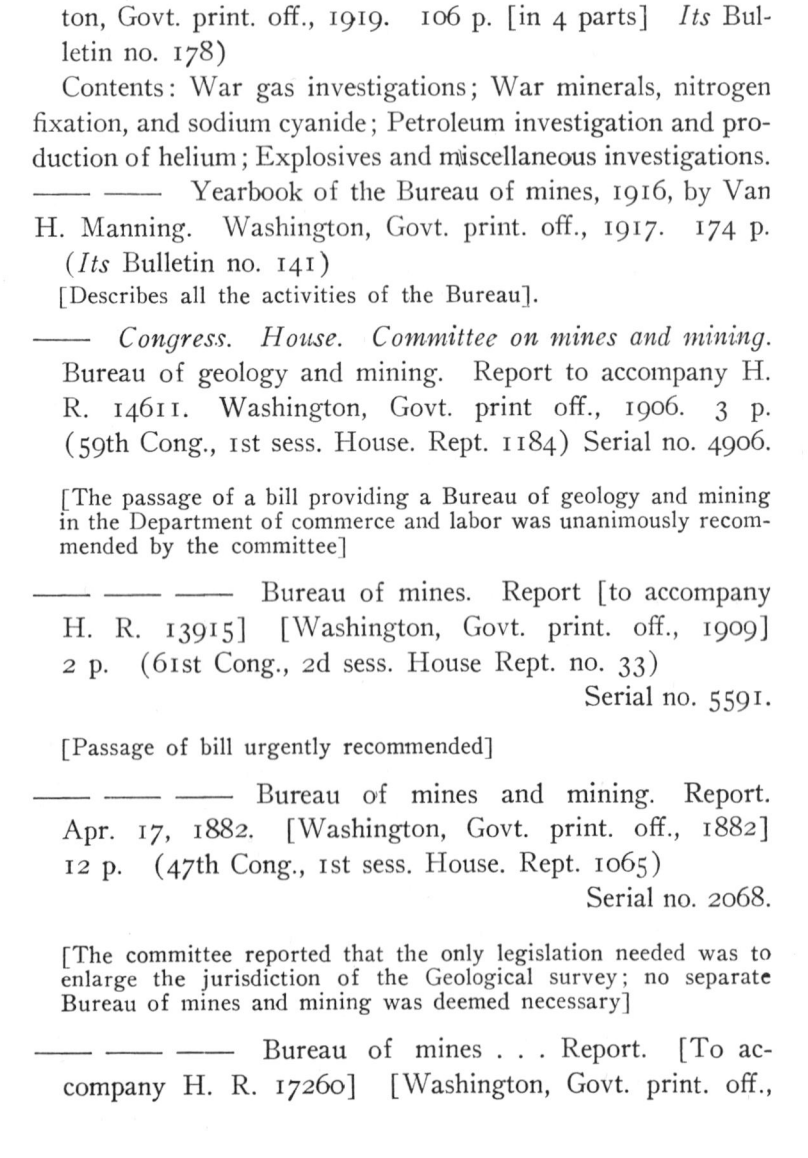

────── ────── War work of the Bureau of mines. Washington, Govt. print. off., 1919. 106 p. [in 4 parts] *Its* Bulletin no. 178)

Contents: War gas investigations; War minerals, nitrogen fixation, and sodium cyanide; Petroleum investigation and production of helium; Explosives and miscellaneous investigations.

────── ────── Yearbook of the Bureau of mines, 1916, by Van H. Manning. Washington, Govt. print. off., 1917. 174 p. (*Its* Bulletin no. 141)

[Describes all the activities of the Bureau].

────── *Congress. House. Committee on mines and mining.* Bureau of geology and mining. Report to accompany H. R. 14611. Washington, Govt. print off., 1906. 3 p. (59th Cong., 1st sess. House. Rept. 1184) Serial no. 4906.

[The passage of a bill providing a Bureau of geology and mining in the Department of commerce and labor was unanimously recommended by the committee]

────── ────── ────── Bureau of mines. Report [to accompany H. R. 13915] [Washington, Govt. print. off., 1909] 2 p. (61st Cong., 2d sess. House Rept. no. 33)

Serial no. 5591.

[Passage of bill urgently recommended]

────── ────── ────── Bureau of mines and mining. Report. Apr. 17, 1882. [Washington, Govt. print. off., 1882] 12 p. (47th Cong., 1st sess. House. Rept. 1065)

Serial no. 2068.

[The committee reported that the only legislation needed was to enlarge the jurisdiction of the Geological survey; no separate Bureau of mines and mining was deemed necessary]

────── ────── ────── Bureau of mines . . . Report. [To accompany H. R. 17260] [Washington, Govt. print. off.,

BIBLIOGRAPHY

1912] 7 p. (62d Cong., 2nd sess. House. Rept. 243)

Serial no. 6129.

U. S. *Congress. House. Committee on mines and mining.* Establishing Bureau of mines in Interior department. Report. [To accompany H. R. 20883] [Washington, 1908] 2 p. (60th Cong., 1st sess. House. Rept. no. 1453)

Serial no. 5226.

[Recommends passage of the bill]

――― ――― ――― Hearings before the Committee on mines and mining . . . of the House of Representatives to consider the question of the establishment of a Bureau of mines . . . March 9 . . . 12 . . . 23 . . . 30, 1908. Washington, Govt. print. off., 1908. 140 p.

[W. F. Englebright, chairman of subcommittees in charge of hearings]

――― ――― ――― Hearings before the subcommittee . . . to consider the question of the establishment of a Bureau of Mines. Mar. 9 . . . 1908. [Washington, Govt. print. off., 1908] 54 p.

――― ――― ――― Mines and mining. Hearing . . . Dec. 4, 1913. [H. bill 6063 and 3988] Washington, Govt. print. off., 1913. 19 p.

[Reference to mining experiment stations]

――― ――― ――― Mines and mining. Hearings . . .April 28 and May 2, 1914. [H. R. 15869] Washington, Govt. print. off., 1914. 39 p.

[The bill provides for mining experiment and mine safety stations]

――― ――― ――― Mining-experiment and mine-safety stations. Report. [to accompany H. R. 15869] [Washington, Govt. print. off., 1914] 28 p. (63d Cong., 2d sess. House Rept. no. 694) Serial no. 6559.

[To establish 10 mining experiment stations . . . and 15 movable mine-safety stations for rescue cars]

――― ――― ――― Mining experiment station in Colorado.

Hearings before the Committee on mines and mining, House of representatives, Monday, December 18, 1911 [and Thursday, January 11, 1912] Washington, Govt. print. off., 1912. 29 p., II, 31-48 p.

—— —— *Senate. Committee on mines and mining.* Bureau of mines. Hearing . . . on H. R. 17260, an act to amend an act entitled "An act to establish in the Department of the Interior a Bureau of mines" . . . June 12, 1912. Washington, Govt. print. off., 1912. 19 p.

[Bill proposes more adequate provisions for the metal-mining interests]

U. S. *Congress. Senate. Committee on mines and mining.* Bureau of mines . . . Report. [To accompany H. R. 13915] . . . [Washington, Govt. print. off., 1910] 41 p. (61st Cong., 2d sess. Senate, Rept. 353) Serial no. 5583.

—— —— —— Bureau of mines . . . Report. (To accompany H. R. 17260) Washington, Govt. print. off., 1912. 13 p. (62d Cong., 2d sess. Senate. Rept. 951) Serial no. 6122.

—— —— —— Establishing Bureau of mines in Interior department . . . Report. [To accompany H. R. 20883] [Washington, Govt. print. off., 1908] 27 p. (60th Cong., 1st sess. Senate. Rept. 692) Serial no. 5219.

[Recommends passage of bill]

—— —— *Select committee on reconstruction and production.* Hearings . . . Washington, Govt. print. off., 1921. 2361 p.

[Statement of Mr. George S. Pope, chief engineer of the Government fuel yard, Washington, D. C., p. 2063–80.]

—— *Dept. of the interior.* Bureau of mines. Letter from the Secretary of the Treasury, transmitting estimates for appropriations for the Bureau of mines for the fiscal year ending June 30, 1911. [Washington, Govt. print. off., 1910] 5 p. (61st Cong., 2d sess. House. Doc. 935)

Serial no. 5836.

―― ―― Work of the Bureau of mines in states west of the Mississippi River. Letter from the Secretary . . . transmitting . . . information relative to the work of the Bureau of mines for the metal-mining industries in states west of the Mississippi River. June 5, 1912. [Washington, Govt. print. off., 1912] 8 p. (62d Cong., 2d sess. Senate Doc. no. 762) Serial no. 6178.

―― *Geological survey.* Division of mines and mining, United States Geological survey. Letter from the Director . . . transmitting a report on joint resolution (S. R. 205) to provide for a division of mines and mining in the United States Geological survey. [Washington, Govt. print. off., 1898] 12 p. (55th Cong., 3d sess. Senate. Doc. no. 40) Serial no. 3378.

[Director thinks a division or Bureau of mines should be established]

―― *Laws, statutes, etc.* An act to establish in the Department of the interior a Bureau of mines. [Public -no. 179. H. R. 13915] Approved, May 16, 1910. 2 p.

―― ―― An act to provide for the establishment and maintenance of mining experiment and mine safety stations for making investigations and disseminating information among employees in mining, quarrying, metallurgical, and other mineral industries, and for other purposes. [Public -no. 283- 63d Congress. H. R. 15869] Approved, Mar. 3, 1915. 1 p.

―― ―― Mining bureau [An act authorizing the establishment of a bureau for mining the precious metals, and providing for its inauguration and support. [Washington, 1869?] 26 p.

Unofficial Publications

American mining congress. Resolution no. 1 (Introduced by E. R. Buckley) for the establishment of a National bureau of mines. (*In its* Proceedings, 1909. Denver, 1909. p. 36)

Bartlett, George A. Federal legislation as it affects the mining industry. (*In* American mining congress. Proceedings, 1909. Denver, 1909. p. 168-73)

[Urges establishment of a Bureau of mines]

Clement, J. K. The work of the chemical laboratories of the Bureau of mines. 1911. 9 p.

[Reprinted from the Journal of industrial and engineering chemistry, v. 3, no. 2. Feb. 1911]

Englebright, W. F. A federal bureau of mines (*In* American mining congress. Proceedings, 1909. Denver,] 1909. p. 162-7)

Foster, M. D. The federal government and the mining industry. (*In* American mining congress. Proceedings, 1913. Denver, 1914. p. 370-4)

[Work of the Bureau of mines]

Holmes, J. A. The Bureau of mines and its work. (*In* American mining congress. Proceedings, 1910. Denver, 1910. p. 219-27)

[Address of the Director of the U. S. Bureau of mines]

——— The national phases of the mining industry. (*In* International congress of applied chemistry. Proceedings. Washington, 1912 [Concord, N. H.] 1912-13. v. 26: 733-50)

[Some reference to the functions of the Bureau of mines]

——— Statement . . . concerning the work and plans of the Bureau of mines. (*In* American mining congress. Proceedings, 1912. Denver [1912] p. 118-9)

International mining congress. [Discussion relative to a Department of mines and mining] (*In its* Proceedings, 1898. Salt Lake City, 1898. p. 152-8)

Manning, Van H. What the Bureau of mines is doing and hopes to do for the metalliferous mining industry. (*In*

BIBLIOGRAPHY

American mining congress. Proceedings, 1915. Washington, 1916. p. 103-13)

Mine inspectors institute of the United States of America. Department of the Interior, Bureau of mines, demonstrations and exhibitions. Thursday, June 11, 1914. Program (*In its* Convention book of the seventh annual meeting. Pittsburgh, 1914. p 5-7)

——— Visit to the U. S. Bureau of mines station and mine; program. (*In* American mining congress. Proceedings, 1914. Pittsburgh, 1914. p. 130-2)

Paul, James W. Mine rescue and first aid operations. (*In* American mining congress. Proceedings, 1913. Denver, 1914. p. 281-7)

[Includes description of the work of the Bureau of mines in reducing mine accidents]

Walcott, C. D. The work of the United States Geological survey in relation to the mineral resources of the United States. (*In* American institute of mining engineers. Transactions, 1901. New York, 1901. p. 3-26)

[Recommends a Division of mines and mining in the Geological survey, to be changed later, if deemed desirable, to a Department of mines and mining]

Walsh, Thomas F. Letter to the Committee on mines and mining . . . favoring establishment of a Bureau of mines and mining and referring to the importance of the development and production of the rarer metals . . . n.p. [1908] 4 p.

Periodical Articles

Assistance in expanding our coal trade by Bureau of mines. Mining and engineering world. Sept. 19, 1914, v.41:537.

[Summarizes a bulletin printed in Spanish, Portugese and English, which describes the various coals of the country available for foreign shipment]

The Bureau of mines act. Engineering and mining journal, Mar. 22, 1913, 95:625.

[Essential features of the law]

Bureau of mines and a new problem. Survey, Aug. 16, 1913, v.30:628-9.

[Plans of the Mine sanitation section recently organized]

Bureau of mines and American radium production. Metallurgical and chemical engineering, Sept. 15, 1916, v.15: 275-6.

[Coöperative work of the Bureau of mines and the National radium institute]

The Bureau of mines as a national force. Coal age, Oct. 11, 1913, v.4:543-4.

[Article states that the "Bureau of mines has obtained a most commanding position largely because of its diplomatic combination of mere scientific research with institutional activity"]

Bureau of mines coöperative work with states proving successful. Mining congress journal, Aug. 1915, v.1: 374.

Bureau of mines exhibit one of Fair's features. Mining congress journal, June, 1915, v.1: p. 265-6.

["Bureau's exhibit at Panama-Pacific exposition the banner display"]

Bureau of mines library contains 11,000 volumes. Mining congress journal, Nov., 1916, v.2:500.

[The main library in Washington is a clearing house for its various branches, giving practical service to eight branches under supervision of the main library]

Bureau of mines reorganized. *Chart.* Engineering and mining journal, Aug. 2, 1919, v. 108: 192.

[Shows divisions into investigations and operations branches]

[Chamberlain, T. C.] Are there line fences in science? Journal of geology, Nov. 1910, v.18: 764-76.

[Concerns the Bureau of mines and its inquiry into protection of life against preventable disaster]

Coal mining investigations. Coal age, Aug. 11- Sept. 1, 1917, v.12:240-1, 276-8, 318-9, 364-7.

BIBLIOGRAPHY

Cottrell, F. G. Relation of the Bureau of mines to the oil industry. Engineering and mining journal, Oct. 2, 1920. v.110:678-9.

──── What the Bureau of mines purposes to do on behalf of the coal industry. *illus.* Coal age, Oct. 7, 1920, v.18: 731-5.

Dedication of the Pittsburgh experiment station of the Bureau of mines. Scientific monthly, Nov. 1919, v.9:476-8.

The destiny of the Bureau of mines. Engineering and mining journal, May 22, 1920, v.109:149-50.

[It will develop along inherited lines, viz., that of a laboratory organization]

Eddy, Lewis H. Mine-rescue car in California. Engineering and mining journal, Nov. 14, 1914, v.98:867-8.

[The trip through California of U. S. Mine-rescue car No. 5 is described, and good results set forth]

English technical papers profuse in compliments, [for the U. S. Bureau of mines and the Geological survey] Mining congress journal, Oct., 1915, v.1:543-4.

Enlarged activites of Bureau of mines [metallurgical work in 1916] Iron age, Nov. 15, 1917, v.100:1194-5.

First aid work, war preparation. Coal age, Oct. 30, 1915, v.8:726.

[Director of Bureau of mines says that "in 48 hours, 50,000 trained first-aid-to-the-injured experts could be mobilized in the great mining states of the country [from] trained mine-rescue crews"]

Geological survey and Bureau of mines assets in case of war. Mining congress journal, April, 1916, v.2:161-4.

Government's safety-first train being visited by 50,000 weekly. Bureau of mines exhibit, which occupies an entire car attracting popular attention. Mining congress journal, June, 1916, v.2:269.70.

Grier, C. D. Electric furnace laboratory of the Bureau of mines [at Seattle station]. *illus.* Chemical and metallurgical engineering, Oct. 29, 1919, v.21:574-6.

Holmes, J. A. The work of the United States Bureau of mines. American labor legislation review, Feb. 1912, v.2:125-30.

Hood, O. P. Fuel conservation by the Bureau of mines; with discussion. American society of mechanical engineers. Journal, April, 1918, v.40:308-10.

Improvised mine fires on an experimental scale. Scientific American supplement, Mar. 21, 1914, v.77:188.

["The Bureau of mines has installed at its Pittsburgh experiment station, an underground chamber, or furnace, in which to carry on experiments relating to mine fires and spontaneous combustion as ocurring in mines"]

Lynott, W. A. Bureau of mines studies of occupational diseases. Journal of industrial and engineering chemistry, Nov. 1916, v.8:1062-4.

[Symposium of important studies of occupational diseases among miners and metallurgical workers]

Manning, Van. H. The Bureau of mines in 1915. Coal age, Jan. 15, 1916, v. 9: 128-9.

["A summary of results obtained by the Bureau in 1915 along lines of safety and efficiency. Coal dust, portable electric mine lamps, breathing apparatus and electricity were investigated carefully, while explosives were the subject of minute research"]

—— Coal industry and the Bureau of mines. Coal age, Jan. 15, 1920, v. 17: 80-1.

—— Coal-mining work of the Bureau of mines in 1916. Coal age, Jan. 13, 1917, v. 11: 106-7.

—— Development of gas warfare work by the Bureau of mines. American institute of mining engineers. Bulletin. Sept. 1918, v.141: sup.xi-xiii.

—— Hazards to men increase as mines become larger and employ more men. Mining congress journal, April, 1916, v.2:169-73.

[References in address to work of Bureau of mines in reducing accidents]

—— Principal achievements of Bureau of mines during

year summed up. Mining congress journal, Jan. 1917, v. 3: 17-18.

[Concise summing up of the work of the year in annual report]

—— Work of the Bureau of mines during 1918. Coal age, Jan. 16, 1919, v.15:105-7.

Methods of testing explosives. Coal age, Nov. 4, 1911, v.1:114-9.

Mine experiments stations named. Engineering and mining journal. Aug. 12, 1916, v.102:294.

[The first two experiment stations will be situated at Fairbanks, Alaska, and at Tucson, Arizona]

Mitchell, G. E. The new Bureau of mines. World today, Oct. 1910, v.19:1150-5; Steam shovel and dredge, Oct., 1910, v.14:851-4.

Moore, R. B. Low temperature laboratory of the Bureau of mines. Science, Nov. 19, 1920, n.s.52:483-4.

National bureau of mines. New England engineer, Nov., 1909, v.2:17.

[Resolution adopted by the American mining congress]

National mine safety demonstrations. Coal age, Oct, 1911-Mar., 1912, v.1:48, 49, 57, 91, 110, 122, 124, 129, 149, 285, 286, 445, 518, 676.

[Description of demonstration at Pittsburgh plant]

The new Bureau of mines. American mining congress. Monthly bulletin, Mar. 1913, v.16: no. 3, p. 35-8.

New work of the Bureau of mines [in metal-mining regions] Engineering and mining journal, March 17, 1917, v. 103: 450-1.

Oil industry of United States saved $50,000,000 by an appropriation of $35,000. Mining congress journal, Nov. 1916, v.2:479-80.

["Hostility which marked entrance of Bureau of mines into oil fields disappears when the logic of its conservation policy becomes evident—ambitious oil program being carried out by Bureau"]

Page, A. W. Safety first underground: new Bureau of mines and its life saving campaign. World's work, Mar., 1912, v.23:549-63.

Parker, D. J. Government mine-rescue cars. Coal age, Oct. 20, 1917, v.12:678-81.

Parsons, C. L. On the extraction of radium, etc., by the U. S. Bureau of mines. Journal of industrial and engineering chemistry. May, 1916, v.8:469-73.

[Reply to letter of C. H. Viol in the March issue of the Journal]

Parsons, C. L., Moore, R. B. [*and others*]. Extraction and recovery of radium, uranium and vanadium from carnotite. Journal of industrial and engineering chemistry. Jan. 1916, v.8: 48-53.

[Describes methods used in coöperative investigation of the Bureau of mines and the National radium institute in extracting radium]

Pittsburgh experiment station of the Bureau of mines. Science, April 10, 1914, v.39: 527-9.

[Plans for the proposed $500,000 experiment station of the U. S. Bureau of mines to be located at Pittsburgh, Pa.]

Pope, George S. Bureau of mines would supervise use of government fuel . . . [statement] before Committee on mines and mining of the House of representatives. (Mining congress journal, Mar. 1917. v.3:92-3).

Proposed gasoline specifications of Bureau of mines. Metallurgical and chemical engineering, Nov. 15, 1916, v.15: 557-9.

[Tentative specifications prepared at request of General supply committee of the executive departments of the federal government . . . for specifications to govern the purchase of gasoline in the District of Columbia]

Raymond, R. W. Proposed bureau of safety in the Department of labor. Engineering and mining journal, Nov. 21, 1914, v.98: 903-4.

[Article opposes changes as liable to affect adversely the work of the Bureau of mines]

Reynolds, W. H. Is the Mines bureau worth while? Coal age, Dec. 21, 1912, v.2:874-6.

[Author thinks criticism of Bureau of mines is unjustified and harmful to the bureau]

Saving human life in mines; the work of the United States Bureau of mines. Scientific American supplement, April 29, 1911, v.71:264-5.

[Description of the life-saving service for the rescue of miners in time of disaster; the oxygen helmet; ambulance car; hospital car]

Shields, M. J. Illustrations of first-aid work. Coal age, Nov. 4, 1911, v.1:120-2.

["Describing in detail the most approved methods of treating injured miners. The illustrations present actual work performed in the government mine at Bruceton, Pennsylvania"]

Spurr, J. E. Reconstruction and post-war work of the Bureau of mines as regards metal mining. Mining congress journal, Dec. 1918, v.4:473-5.

Sundry civil bill increases appropriation for Bureau of mines $207,705. Makes total for bureau close to $1,000,000. Mining congress journal, June, 1916, v.2:267.

Taylor, G. R. Underground America: the Bureau of mines and its work of salvage and invention. Survey, Feb. 5, 1916, v.35:547-53.

Technicians in government service. War minerals investigation committee. Engineering and mining journal, Feb. 1, 1919, v.107:225-6.

Tucson, Arizona, and Fairbanks, Alaska, get mining experiment stations. Mining congress journal, Aug. 1916, v.2:355-6.

[Two of the three mining experiment stations . . . provided for by Congress. Under direction of Bureau of mines]

Two important discoveries by Chemistry department, Bureau of mines. Mining and engineering world, Mar. 13, 1915, v.42:499.

[Account of Dr. Walter F. Rittman's discoveries with regard to gasoline and toluol and benzol]

Unconditional coöperation with Bureau of mines promised in West. Mining congress journal, Nov. 1915, v.1:589.

The U. S. Bureau of mines. Engineering magazine, July, 1910, v.39:581-2.

[A critical discussion of its purpose, powers, and influence]

The U. S. Bureau of mines. Some good things it has accomplished, as shown in its second annual report. Colliery engineer, Feb. 1913, v.33:380–1.

Urge coöperation with the Bureau of mines. Mining congress journal, Mar. 1916, v.2:117.

[Committee report of United mine workers of America]

Viol, C. H. Remarks on production of radium by the Bureau of mines. Journal of industrial and engineering chemistry. Mar., and July, 1916, v.8:284-6; 660-2.

[Charges misstatements in the public press with regard to the work of the Bureau of mines in the production of radium, etc.]

Williams, H. S. Staged mine explosion. Hearst's magazine, May, 1912, v.21:2281-2.

Work and purpose of mining bureau. Coal age, Nov. 4, 1911, v.1:102–8.

[Describes methods used in coöperative investigation of the Bureau of mines]

Work of the Bureau of mines. Metallurgical and chemical engineering, Jan. 19, 1917, v.16:111-13.

Scrap book [of the Bureau of mines] 1914—.

[Volumes for each year—consist of press clippings relating to the Bureau of mines]

INDEX

Accidents, investigation and prevention of, 3-6, 8-11, 13-14, 16, 44; statistics of, 16, 43.
Administration, general, 39-45.
Alaska, inspection of coal mines in, 5, 47.
Assistant Director, powers and duties of, 39, 45.
Assistant to the Director, powers and duties of, 39.

Chief Clerk, powers and duties of, 40-41.
Chief Surgeon, powers and duties of, 46.
Coal, investigation and testing of, 2-4, 22-25, 48-49.
Coöperative relations, 7, 19-20, 21, 27, 29-33.

Director, appointment of, 37; compensation of, 37; powers and duties of, 39; qualifications of, 37.
Districts, mining, 47; safety, 44-45.

Education and Information, Division of, 41-43.
Electricity, promotion of safe use of, 5-6, 10-11.
Equipment, investigation and testing of, 4, 6, 8, 10-11, 16-18, 46-47, 49.
Experimental mine, 9-10, 81.
Explosions, investigation and prevention of, 3, 4, 8-10, 16, 44.

Explosives, investigation and testing of, 3-5, 9-10, 16, 17, 33, 46.

Fees, for investigations, 5, 138-9.
Field offices, 6, 48, 50, 79-81.
Fire-prevention, 6, 16, 26.
First-aid, training in, 3, 12, 15, 44.
Fuels, testing of, 5, 24, 27.
Fuels Division, 48-49.

Gas, natural, investigation of, 25, 26, 48, 49.
Geological Survey, mining technological work of, 1-4; coöperation with, 18, 24, 28.
Government Fuel Yard, operation of, 34-35, 45, 77-78.

Hygiene, promotion of, 1, 5, 11-13, 19, 33, 43.

Indian Affairs, Office of, coöperation with, 19, 32.
Inspector of coal mines for Alaska, 5, 47.
Interior, Secretary of, may authorize tests on a fee basis, 5, 139; may requisition additional copies of publications, 75.
Investigations Branch, 45-50.

Leasing Act, administration of regulations under, 32-33, 139.
Lignite, investigation of, 23, 49.

Metallurgical Division, 48.
Metalurgy, investigations in, 4-6, 7, 21, 48.

161

INDEX

Mine inspection in Alaska, 5, 31-32.
Mine leases, inspection of, 32-33.
Mine-Rescue Cars and Stations, Division of, 43-45.
Mine-safety cars, 13-15, 44-45, 78-82.
Mineral Technology, Division of, 47-48.
Mineral technology, investigations in, 4-6, 20-21, 47-48.
Mining Division, 44, 46-47.
Mining experiment stations, 6, 20, 43, 47, 49-50, 78-82.
Mining Experiment Stations, Division of, 49-50.
Mining laws, compilations of, 35.
Mining methods, investigation of, 4-6, 7, 16-20, 46-47.

Office Administration, Division of, 39-41.
Operations Branch, 39-45.

Peat, investigation of, 5, 23, 49.
Petroleum and Natural Gas, Division of, 49.
Petroleum, investigation and testing of, 25-29, 48, 49.
Public Health Service, coöperation with, 12-13, 46.
Publications, 15-16, 18, 27, 35, 42, 73-76.

Quarry methods, investigation of, 18, 46.

Radium investigations, 20-21.

Safety, promotion of, 1-11, 16-20, 33, 43-45, 46, 49.
Specifications for fuel, 2, 24, 27-9.
Standards, Bureau of, structural materials work assumed by, 5; coöperation with, 18.
Statistics, of accidents, 16, 43; of explosives, 43; of petroleum and petroleum products, 27.

War Minerals Relief Commission, coöperation with, 34.
War work, 20, 22, 28, 33-34, 35-36.